THE
PORTLAND
VASE

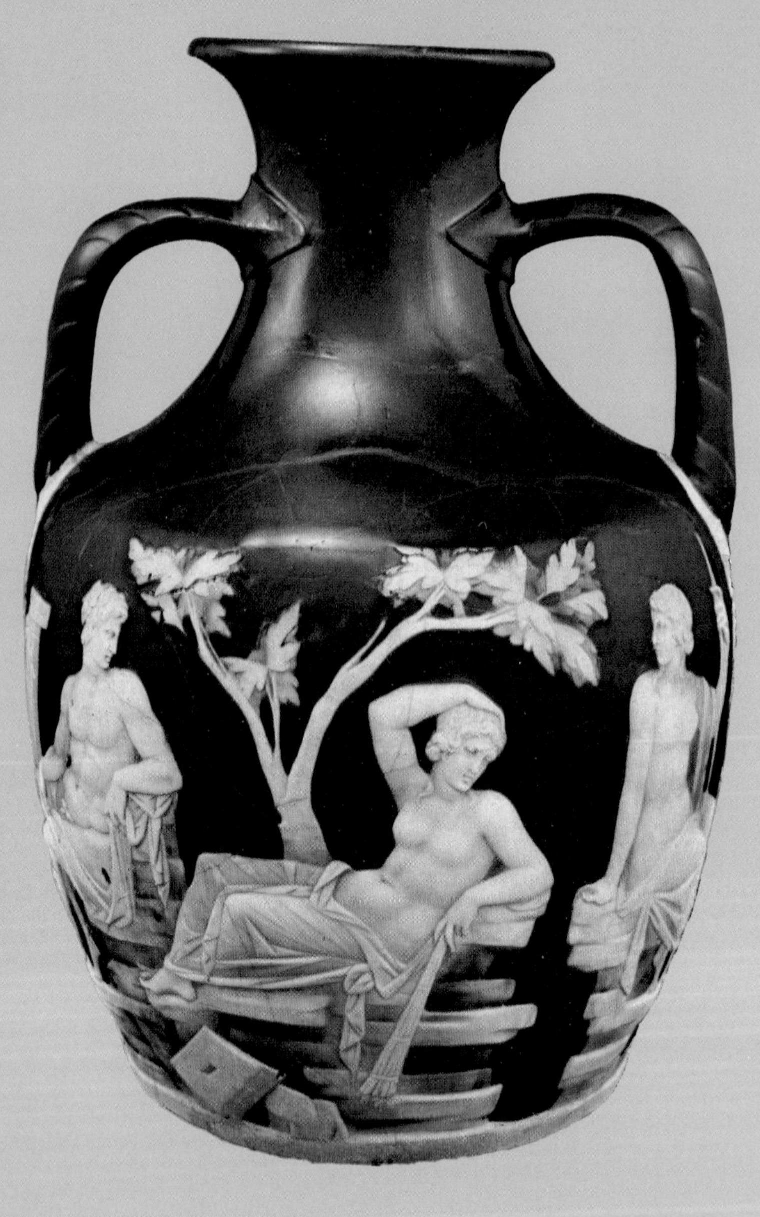

The Portland Vase, figures E—G

THE PORTLAND VASE

D. E. L. HAYNES

Or bid Mortality rejoice and mourn
O'er the fine forms on PORTLAND'S *mystic urn.*
Erasmus Darwin, *The Botanic Garden*, Canto II, 319

PUBLISHED FOR
THE TRUSTEES OF THE BRITISH MUSEUM
BY
BRITISH MUSEUM PUBLICATIONS LIMITED

*Printed in Great Britain
at the University Press, Oxford
by Vivian Ridler
Printer to the University*

LIST OF ILLUSTRATIONS

The letter-references for the figures on the vase
are given on the drawing inside back cover

ACKNOWLEDGMENTS

The writer is grateful to the Harvard University Press for permission to quote from the Loeb Classical Library edition of *Hesiod, the Homeric Hymns and Homerica* (London, 1914) Hugh G. Evelyn-White's translation of Hesiod frag. 58; to Professor Alfonso de Franciscis, Director of the Museo Nazionale, Naples, for permission to use the photograph of the Pompeian Blue Vase reproduced in Pl. XII; and to Miss M. O. Miller for making the drawing of the frieze of the Portland Vase reproduced at the end of the book

INTRODUCTION

'EXCEPT THE APOLLO BELVEDERE, the Niobes, and two or three others of the first-class marbles, I do not believe that there are any monuments of antiquity existing that were executed by so great an artist.' So Sir William Hamilton writing of the Portland Vase in 1786. Since then the archaeological discoveries of the nineteenth century have opened our eyes to classical Greek art; and works of the Roman period, to which, as we can now see, both the vase and the Apollo Belvedere belong, no longer receive such uncritical admiration as they did in Hamilton's day. Yet even if beside, say, the frieze of the Parthenon, the Portland Vase seems to shine with a borrowed, lunar light, it is still an object in which unprejudiced eyes will find much beauty. Moreover, it is not beauty alone which has kept interest in it alive. The subject of its frieze is an enigma which has challenged and defied three centuries of classical scholarship. The virtuosity of its workmanship has inspired modern craftsmen, including the great Josiah Wedgwood, to imitation. And lastly its long and eventful history, in the course of which it has been associated with a number of unusual people, makes it a fascinating minor document in the 'proper study of mankind'.

HISTORY

How or when the vase was discovered, we do not know. When we first hear of it,[1] it was in the possession of the liberal and art-loving Cardinal Francesco Maria del Monte (1549–1627), in whose Roman residence, the Palazzo Madama, it was seen by the Provençal scholar de Peiresc (1580–1637) in the winter of 1600–01. The vase must have made a deep impression on de Peiresc, for twenty-four years later, when he and Rubens were planning a work on Roman cameos, he hoped to be allowed to include it

[1]For the earliest recorded history of the Portland Vase see now H. Möbius in *Kölner Jahrbuch für Vor- und Frühgeschichte*, Vol. IV, 1967/68, pp. 25 f.

and only gave up the idea when he heard that permission to publish it had already been granted to the celebrated Italian antiquarian Cassiano dal Pozzo (1578–1657). Shortly afterwards de Peiresc received, presumably as a present from Cardinal del Monte, a lead cast of the vase, from which he commissioned Ambroise Fredeau of Toulouse to paint a grisaille for his house at Boysgency. The cast itself he passed on later to Rubens, who was delighted to receive this copy of 'a most noble monument of antiquity'.

Cardinal del Monte had originally intended to leave his vase to a certain 'Monsieur', probably Henri II of Condé; but in the course of a long illness he was persuaded by his family to change his mind in their favour; and after his death in 1627 his heirs sold it for 600 scudi to Cardinal Francesco Barberini, the nephew of Pope Urban VIII. So from the Palazzo Madama the vase came to the Palazzo Barberini, the splendid new palace then being built for the Pope and Cardinal Barberini on the Quirinal hill. The Cardinal's acquisition must have gratified one member of his household in particular, Cassiano dal Pozzo, whose interest in the vase we have already noted; and six sketches of it are to be found in his celebrated *Museum Chartaceum*, an extensive collection of drawings from the antique now divided between the Royal Library at Windsor and the British Museum (Pl. XIV). But his proposed publication came to nothing; and in the event the first person to make the vase more widely known was Bernardino Capitelli, who engraved the frieze in 1633 (Appendix No. 1).

Nine years later appeared the *Aedes Barberinae* of Girolamo Teti, Cardinal Barberini's librarian, a panegyric description of the Palazzo Barberini and its contents, in which the vase is discussed at length (Appendix No. 2). Interpreting the frieze as a symbolic representation of the life and death of the Roman emperor Alexander Severus (A.D. 222–235), Teti conjectured that the vase had originally been that emperor's cinerary urn, a theory which must have greatly enhanced its prestige, for in the eyes of counter-reformation Rome Alexander Severus was a paragon of virtue, almost a pagan saint. Teti's conjecture was also pretty certainly the origin of the story, universally accepted as true in the eighteenth and nineteenth centuries, that the vase was discovered in a marble sarcophagus excavated in 1582 under the

Monte del Grano on the southern outskirts of Rome. This story, which first appears in Pietro Santi Bartoli's *Gli Antichi Sepolcri*, 1697 (Appendix No. 4), is evidently no more than a clumsy attempt to combine Teti's fantasy with the equally wild claim of the finders of the sarcophagus that the two carved figures on its lid represented Alexander Severus and his mother Julia Mamaea. Flaminio Vacca, who has left us a contemporary account of the finding of the sarcophagus in his *Memorie*, 1594, says nothing of the discovery of a vase within it; yet he could hardly have failed to mention so conspicuous an object if it had been there.[2]

Bartoli's work was one of three which spread the fame of the vase throughout Europe, the other two being de la Chausse's *Romanum Museum*, 1690 (Appendix No. 3) and Montfaucon's *L'Antiquité expliquée*, 1722 (Appendix No. 5). By the middle of the eighteenth century there can have been few cultured Europeans who had not heard of it. By now, however, the fortunes of the Barberini family were beginning to decline, a process accelerated in the latter part of the century by the heavy losses incurred at cards by Donna Cornelia Barberini-Colonna, Princess of Palestrina and the last of her line. At all events, by about 1780 the Princess had made up her mind that the vase must be sold. She found a ready purchaser in James Byres, a Scotsman resident in Rome, in whom the callings of artist, antiquarian and dealer were equivocally combined. It seems likely that Byres only bought the vase in order to sell it again; but during his brief ownership he commissioned the noted gem-engraver Pichler to take a mould from it; and from this mould James Tassie subsequently cast sixty plaster copies, one of which is now in the British Museum (Pls. X and XI). After the copies had been made the mould was broken on Byres' instructions.

Byres must have sold the vase not later than 1783. The buyer was Sir William Hamilton, British Ambassador to the Court of Naples and a passionate collector of classical antiquities. 'The person I bought it of at Rome', he later wrote to Wedgwood, 'will do me the justice to say that the superior excellence of this exquisite masterpiece of ancient art struck me so much at first sight, that I eagerly asked, "Is it yours? Will you sell it?" He

[2] See H. Stuart Jones in *Athenaeum*, London, 27 Feb., 1909, p. 265.

answered, "Yes, but never under £1000". "I will give you a thous-
and pounds" and so I did, though God knows it was not very
convenient for me at that moment'.[3]

Hamilton had obviously allowed his collector's zeal to run
away with him. Unable to pay Byres in cash, he gave him a bond
bearing interest at 5%; and in August, 1783, we find the Ambassador back in London, having brought the vase with him,
evidently in the hope of selling it. The embarrassment of having to
cry his own wares was, however, spared him. His niece, Mary
Hamilton, was a close friend of the Dowager Duchess of Portland,
whom he was presently invited to visit at Bulstrode Park.
Hamilton must have said enough about the vase on this occasion
to whet the Duchess's appetite, for shortly after his visit she let it
be known that she wished to see the object itself. Accordingly, on
31st December, 1783, when she was next in London, Hamilton
waited on her with the vase, the sight of which confirmed her in
her determination to acquire it for her famous museum of natural
and artificial curiosities at her residence in Privy Gardens,
Whitehall. The negotiations for purchase, in which Mary
Hamilton acted as a go-between, were conducted with the con-
trived intrigue of a contemporary comedy; but by the middle
of January, 1784, the matter was virtually settled: Hamilton, who
confessed to his niece that his financial position left him little
option but to sell, had consented to part with the vase and four
lesser antiquities for 1800 guineas. The Duchess, for her part,
agreed not to disturb an existing arrangement whereby the artist
Cipriani was to make a drawing of the vase to be engraved by
Bartolozzi. It was thus some months before the Duchess saw her
new treasure safely installed in the Portland Museum (Pl. XV),
but early in June Hamilton writes to his niece: 'I have directed
him (Cipriani) to bring the vase to you and you will be so good as
to convey it secretly to the Duchess. The Queen has desired to see
it, therefore Cipriani is to wait on her Majesty the day before he
brings it to you.'[4]

[3]Letter of July, 1786, quoted by W. Mankowitz *The Portland Vase and its
Copies*, London, 1952, p. 28.
[4]For the purchase negotiations see E. and F. Anson *Mary Hamilton*,
London, 1925 pp. 155-158; *Autobiography and Correspondence of Mrs
Delany* (ed. Lady Llanover), Second Series. London, 1862, Vol. III,
pp. 192-205.

The Duchess—'a simple woman', Horace Walpole called her, 'but perfectly sober, and intoxicated only by *empty* vases' – died in July 1785. In the following spring the Portland Museum was sold at auction by Mr Skinner and Co.; and the vase, which came up as Lot no. 4155 on the 7th June, the thirty-eighth and last day of the sale, went to a Mr Tomlinson for 980 guineas. Tomlinson was rumoured to be acting on behalf of the Duke of Marlborough, but it seems certain that his principal was in fact the Dowager Duchess's son, the third Duke of Portland.[5] At all events, the vase must have been the Duke of Portland's property when a week or so after the sale he agreed to lend it to Wedgwood for twelve months to enable the famous potter to model it for reproduction in his jasper ware. Wedgwood, it appears, had intended to bid for the vase himself and only refrained from doing so because the Duke promised him the loan of it if he were successful.

To the period of the third Duke's ownership must be referred an incident for which our only evidence is a statement in *The Gentleman's Magazine*[6] that the vase had been 'repaired after its fracture by the Duchess of Gordon'. The Duchess in question must be the notorious 'Jenny of Montreith', the 'Flower of Galloway', who married Alexander, Duke of Gordon, in 1767 and died in 1812; for when the Duke married again in 1820 the vase was already in the British Museum. Heavy-handedness was perhaps only natural in one whose youthful pastime it had been to ride down Edinburgh High Street 'on a sow belonging to Peter Ramsay, the stabler in St. Mary's Wynd, and which her sister, afterwards Lady Wallace, thumped lustily behind with a stick'.[7]

It was possibly in the hope of protecting the vase from domestic risks that in 1810 the fourth Duke of Portland decided to deposit it on loan in the British Museum; but here thirty-five years later a disaster befell it far worse than anything it had suffered before. At 3.45 p.m. on 7th February, 1845, a young man entered the Hamiltonian Ante-Room where the vase was kept in a glass case, and picking up a conveniently-placed weapon variously identified

[5]See *The Gentleman's Magazine* Vol. LVI, London, 1786, July-December, p. 744.
[6]New Series Vol. XXIII, 1845, p. 300.
[7]*An autobiographical chapter in the life of Jane, Duchess of Gordon*, Glasgow, 1864, p. v.

as 'a curiosity in sculpture' and 'a Persepolitan monument of basalt' brought it down on top of the case smashing both it and the vase to pieces. On hearing the noise, museum officials hastened to shut off the area and began questioning the visitors present. When they approached the culprit, 'a stout young man, in a kind of pilot coat, with both hands in his pockets before him', he at once confessed and was taken to the Bow Street Police Station, where he gave his name, probably falsely, as William Lloyd, and his address as a coffee-house in Long Acre; he had, it appeared, been a student of Trinity College, Dublin, but was now earning a living as a scene-painter. 'I certainly broke the vase', he admitted to Mr Jardine, the examining magistrate, 'and all I can say in extenuation of my conduct is, that I had been indulging in intemperance for a week before, and was then only partially recovered from the effects which that indulgence had produced upon my mind. I was suffering at the time from a kind of nervous excitement – a continual fear of everything I saw – and it was under this impression, strange as it may seem, that I committed the act for which I was deservedly taken into custody at the Museum'.

The prisoner stood self-convicted; but Mr Jardine found himself in some difficulty when it came to the question of punishment, for owing to an ambiguity in the wording of the Wilful Damage Act it was doubtful whether its provisions could be applied in the case of an object worth more than £5. However, while he was still debating this question, Mr Bodkin for the prosecution pointed out that the prisoner had also broken the glass case in which the vase was displayed, an object worth only £3. Mr Jardine was thus able to find the prisoner guilty on a new charge of breaking the case and imposed a fine of £3 with an alternative of two months hard labour in the House of Correction. Lloyd had only ninepence in the world and was committed to gaol; but two days later a friend paid the fine for him and he was set free.[8]

At first sight the damage to the vase must have appeared irreparable, for it had been broken into more than two hundred

[8]For the whole episode of the breaking of the vase by William Lloyd see *The Times*, February 7 and 12, 1845; *The Gentleman's Magazine*, New Series, Vol. XXIII, 1845, p. 300.

fragments (Pl. XVI); but John Doubleday, the Museum craftsman entrusted with the difficult task of trying to piece them
together, carried it out with such skill that by September 1845 the
vase could again be placed on exhibition. For the next hundred
years it remained continuously on loan in the Museum, apart
from an interval of three years, from 1929 to 1932, during which it
was put up for sale at Messrs. Christie's, but failed to reach the
reserve.[9] In 1945 the purchase of the vase by the British Museum
with funds bequeathed by James Rose Vallentin brought the
Portland family's long and generous loan to an end. Three years
later the Museum received from Miss Amy Reeves, executrix of
the late Mr G. H. Gabb, a box containing thirty-seven small chips
of glass said to come from the Portland Vase. According to an
explanation accompanying the gift, the chips were those which
Doubleday had failed to re-incorporate in the vase when he
mended it, and had put aside in a drawer in the Museum. After
his death another Museum vase-mender found them and took
them to Mr Gabb who was commissioned to make a box for them.
But the vase-mender died before the box was ready and, though
Mr Gabb finished it, he apparently forgot to send it and the chips
back to the Museum. After the receipt of Miss Reeves's gift it was
decided to take the vase to pieces again, partly in the hope of
being able to assign some of the chips to their rightful places, but
mainly in order to remove the old glue, which had grown dis-
coloured and obtrusive, and replace it with a colourless modern
adhesive. In the event, only three of the chips could be included,
but there can be no doubt that the reconstruction, which was
undertaken by Mr J. H. W. Axtell, has greatly improved the
general appearance of the vase.

DESCRIPTION

The Portland Vase, which is 9¾ inches (24·5 cm.) high and has a
maximum diameter of 7 inches (17·7 cm.), is made of glass: the
body and handles from a cobalt-blue glass so dark as to be almost
indistinguishable from black except when seen by transmitted

[9] May 2, 1929.

light; the relief from an opaque milky-white glass. The shape has often been criticized as inelegantly squat, even by so confirmed an admirer of the vase's other qualities as Wedgwood[10]; but the abrupt truncation of the lower part of the body is accidental, for the vase has lost its proper base. The glass disc formerly fastened beneath it (Pl. IXa) cannot have belonged to it originally; as we shall see below (pp. 25 f), the disc differs from the vase in colour, style and scale; and to make a level seating for it the bottom of the body has been roughly chipped all round, an improvisation quite out of keeping with the careful workmanship of the rest. There can be little doubt that the original base would have been blown in one piece with the body, though what form it would have taken is less certain. As a two-handled vessel or *amphora*, the vase might have had a flat base with a moulded rim like that of the Auldjo Jug (Pl. XIII), but it is perhaps more likely on the analogy of the closely-related Blue Vase from Pompeii (Pl. XII) that the body tapered downwards to a knob or point. The accident which deprived the vase of its base no doubt also caused the extensive fractures reproduced in Tassie's cast (Pl. XI). When this earliest and unrecorded accident occurred, we do not know: all that can be said with certainty is that the vase had already been repaired with the disc before it was described by Teti in 1642.

The handles are vertically ridged on the outside and cut in V-shaped sections which overlap like sheaths on the stem of a plant. From the lower attachment of each a Pan's mask carved in the white glass of the frieze hangs by its horns; half animal and half human, the goat-god knits his brows in brooding melancholy. The masks divide the figures of the frieze into two groups, one comprising four figures, A–D (the letters refer to the drawing at end of book), the other three, E–G; but the two groups together constitute a single scene[11]: a lover's encounter with his beloved.

The lover, an athletic youth with short, curly hair (A, Pl. III), moves to the right in front of a simple rustic shrine in the Doric style, behind which grows a small-leaved shrub, perhaps a myrtle.

[10]Letter to Sir W. Hamilton of 24 June, 1786, quoted by W. Mankowitz, *op. cit.*, p. 24.

[11]Apart from R. Venuti (Appendix No. 6), L. Polacco (Appendix No. 20) is the only person who has hitherto recognized this crucial fact.

The young man has evidently been lingering by the shrine, probably sitting on its plinth; for the way in which the lower folds of the cloak in his right hand cling round the foot of the nearer pillar proves that he is picking the garment up, not throwing it off. Even now, to judge from his tip-toe gait and slight stoop, he is not altogether sure of himself; but a chubby Eros holding a bow in the left hand and a torch in the right (B, Pl. IV) flies ahead of him, urging him on and glancing backwards to make sure that he follows; and a woman sitting on a low rock in front of him (C, Pl. IV) turns round in her seat and supports him under his left arm with her outstretched right; one would say she has just helped him to his feet. The woman, whose long unruly tresses fall loose on her shoulders, wears a mantle wrapped about her outstretched legs, and her left hand caresses a serpent-like creature which rises fawning towards her face. Though she looks up affectionately at the young man, he does not return her gaze: his eyes are fixed on the god of love who is already passing her by and points with his torch to a goal which lies on the other side of the vase. The last figure on this side is an elderly bearded man (D, Pl. V), who stands in front of the woman with his right foot raised on a rock at the base of the tree (laurel or olive?) under which she sits. He was evidently conversing with her before she turned to help the young lover, but now he too has transferred his attention to the youth, whose approach he watches with pensive expression, supporting his right elbow on his thigh, his chin on the hand, and holding his left arm, round which is wound a cloak, behind his back. Between him and the Pan's mask of the adjacent handle grows another tree, a fig perhaps or a plane.

Of the three figures on the other side of the vase the central is that of a half-draped girl (F, Pl. VII) who reclines on a lofty plat-form of layered rock under a tree: again it is difficult to tell whether a fig or a plane is intended. The girl leans back lightly on her left elbow and rests her right arm languidly across her head, turning her head away from her companions and gazing into the distance as if lost in reverie. The sensuous abandon of her attitude would unmistakably proclaim her the object of the young man's desire, even if we did not find the same pose habitually used in ancient art to represent beauty taken unawares: Ariadne surprised by Dionysus, for example, Rea Silvia by Mars, or Endymion by Luna. The girl's wavy hair is drawn back from her forehead to the nape of her neck, whence two long tresses fall on to her shoulders. From the limp fingers of her left hand an inverted but still burning torch hangs forgotten; and on the ground at her feet lies a square block of stone with chamfered edges and a central slot, apparently a fallen capital.

The girl is framed between a male and a female onlooker who sit on other excrescences of the rock, he at her feet (E, Pl. VI) she at her head (G, Pl. VIII). The two figures are symmetrically composed, each turned away from the centre with one leg drawn back behind the other, and each looking round over the shoulder; but while the man's eyes are directed down at the girl, the woman's level gaze passes over her head, intent, we must presume, on Eros and the oncoming lover. The curly-haired man leans back easily in his rocky seat, resting his left elbow on its back and relaxing his right arm on his thigh. The fingers of his left hand toy with the edge of his cloak which has slipped from his powerful body, leaving only two corners draped over his legs. In the background behind him rises a square pillar crowned by a block-like capital with slotted sides (Pl. XI). The woman, who occupies an isolated, top-heavy-looking pile of rock, holds herself more erect than the man, pressing down with her right hand on the stone as she turns to look behind her, and grasping a tall staff or sceptre in her left. Her legs are draped in a mantle, an end of which is thrown up over her left arm. Though her hair is dressed like the girl's with a knot at the nape and tresses falling on the shoulders, her forms are those of a maturer woman.

IDENTIFICATION OF
THE FIGURES OF THE FRIEZE

At first sight the identification of the figures of the frieze (apart from Eros) might appear difficult, if not impossible, owing to the sparing use which the artist has made of attributes: how varied and fascinating a crop of conjecture his reticence has yielded, will be apparent from the bibliography at the end of this work. Nevertheless, in the serpent-like creature associated with the seated woman on the first side of the vase (C, Pl. IV) he has in fact provided us with the only clue we need to recognize the protagonists of the scene. This creature has sometimes been mistaken for a snake, with which it has in common its sinuous, scaly body and its segmented belly; but the wolf-like head with flat, raking muzzle and protended ears, the long fan-shaped fin hanging from the throat, and the small fins on the back of the neck prove beyond all possible doubt that it is a sea-dragon or *kētos*: no snake was ever represented thus in ancient art. True, *kētē* often have flippers or forepaws, but by no means always[12]; and in any case, what we see here may well be only the creature's neck, its body and limbs being concealed behind the woman's legs.

The mistress of an amiable sea-dragon can only be a sea-goddess; and if in the light of this we look again at her bearded *vis-à-vis* (D, Pl. V), it will surely strike us as significant that his pose is very like that commonly used for Poseidon; he too must be a sea-god of some sort, if not Poseidon himself. Thus the lovers meet under the auspices of a pair of benevolent marine deities, indeed with the active encouragement of one of them; and in the whole repertory of classical mythology there is only one story in which such a situation could arise: the story of the marriage of Peleus and Thetis.

In what is probably the most familiar version of this myth, Zeus and Poseidon both fell in love with the sea-goddess Thetis, daughter of Nereus and Doris; but Themis, the goddess of established order, prophesied that Thetis was destined to bear a son mightier than his father. Fearful for their own supremacy, the two gods readily agreed to Themis' suggestion that Thetis should be married to a mortal, and the choice fell on Peleus, son of Aiakos. The sea-goddess, however, disdained union with a mortal and in order to elude Peleus' advances changed herself into many different things: a lion, a snake, fire, water and so on. Nevertheless, following the advice of his friend the Centaur Chiron, Peleus would not let go, and after a long wrestling-match succeeded in forcing Thetis to resume her original shape and submit to his desire. To celebrate the wedding a feast was held in Chiron's

[12]Not, for example, those associated with Tethys on mosaics from Antioch, D. Levi, *Antioch Mosaic Pavements*, Princeton 1947, Vol. II, Pls. XXXV a, CLVII b.

cave on Mount Pelion in Thessaly, to which all the gods came bearing gifts: and the Muses entertained the company by singing to the accompaniment of Apollo's lyre. Yet the marriage was not a happy one, and after the birth of her son, Achilles, Thetis deserted her husband and returned to her native element.

It has long been recognized that the myth of Peleus and Thetis, as we have just related it, combines material from two different sources; for the dour, polymorphous bride who has to be overcome in a wrestling-match and later runs away, is evidently out of place in the story of a marriage not only ordained by the gods but afterwards hallowed by their presence at the wedding-feast. The wrestling-match belongs, in fact, to a primitive folk-tale common to many Indo-European peoples which tells of a mortal man's unhappy love-affair with a water-nixie; and until it was introduced into Greek epic poetry, the Olympian gods played no part in the story. No doubt it was in order to avoid such incongruity that the wrestling-match was omitted in a second epic version of the myth. According to this version Thetis had been brought up on Mount Olympus by Hera, the wife of Zeus; when, therefore, Zeus made amorous approaches to her, she rejected him out of gratitude to her protectress and fled back into the sea. Thwarted and enraged, the king of the gods vowed that she should be married to a mortal as a punishment; but Hera heard of the oath and reciprocal gratitude prompted her to ensure that the mortal should at least be the best available, which was Peleus. To a husband so highly recommended Thetis did not demur: and Hera herself invited the Olympian gods to the wedding-feast.

From omitting the gloomier folk-tale elements – the violent courtship and the subsequent parting – it was but a short step to presenting the union of Peleus and Thetis as an ideal marriage, at any rate from the bridegroom's point of view; and Hesiod, who wrote in the seventh century B.C., already celebrates it as such. A fragment of his *Catalogue of Women* tells how Peleus returned home after capturing Iolkos bringing his newly-wed bride with him, 'and all the people envied him in their hearts seeing how he had sacked the well-built city and accomplished his joyous marriage; and they all spake this word: "Thrice, yea, four-times blessed son of Aiakos, happy Peleus! For far-seeing Olympian Zeus has given you a wife with many gifts and the blessed gods have brought your marriage fully to pass, and in these halls you go up to the holy bed of a daughter of Nereus. Truly the father, the son of Kronos, made you very pre-eminent among heroes and honoured above other men who eat bread and consume the fruit of the ground." '[13]

The last stage in the development of the myth was to exploit its romantic possibilities at the expense of both folk-tale and epic elements: to transform it, in short, into a bourgeois love-story. There can be little doubt that this transformation was effected in Ptolemaic Alexandria, the birthplace of romantic literature; and although no original Alexandrian poem on the marriage of Peleus and Thetis has come down to us, we almost certainly possess an imitation of such a work in Catullus' famous epyllion, *Carmen* LXIV. The poem tells how, when the Argonauts sailed to fetch the Golden Fleece, the daughters of Nereus emerged from the waves to gaze with wonder on the first ship, and were thus themselves seen by mortal eyes for the first time. Among the Argonauts was Peleus, among the Nereids Thetis, and they fell in love with each other at first sight, a typically Alexandrian motif. As if in defiance of the gloomy tradition of the wrestling-match, Catullus expressly affirms that Thetis did not regard her marriage as a *mésalliance*: 'then it was, they say, that Peleus was fired with love for Thetis; then that Thetis thought it no disgrace to marry a mortal; then that the father himself saw that Peleus must be united with Thetis ... Oft in my song will I call upon you, Peleus, Thessaly's bulwark, whom a fortunate marriage has exalted so conspicuously, to whom Jupiter himself, Jupiter the father of the gods, surrendered his own love. Was it you whom fairest Thetis, the daughter of Nereus, embraced? Was it you to whom Tethys gave her grand-daughter in marriage, and Oceanus too, who girdles the whole earth with sea?'[14] Then the poet goes on to describe the wedding celebrations. First the country-folk come from far and near to admire Peleus' splendid palace at Pharsalus, whose rich appointments include a wonderful coverlet for the bridal bed embroidered with the marriage of Dionysus and Ariadne. Then, after the mortals have withdrawn, the gods arrive to attend the wedding feast, and the Fates sing in honour of the newly married

[13]fr. 58, Loeb ed., London, 1914, p. 187, trans. Hugh G. Evelyn-White.
[14]Catullus, LXIV, 19-21, 24-30.

pair: 'Never before has any house sheltered such loves, never before has love joined two lovers in such a harmonious bond as that which unites Thetis with Peleus, Peleus with Thetis.'[15]

A romantic version of the myth close to that which inspired Catullus' poem must lie behind the frieze of the Portland Vase.[16] Carrying a torch to guide her through the night, Thetis has emerged from the sea on the coast of Thessaly and lain down on a rocky couch in her sanctuary, to which she often resorted.[17] But on this occasion Peleus has been waiting for her, seated on her shrine; and after a moment's hesitation, not unnatural in a mortal pretender to a goddess's hand, he steps forward, emboldened not only by Eros, but by Thetis' own kin; for the sea-goddess who supports him under the arm, must be either Doris, the mother of Thetis, or Tethys, her grandmother; the bearded sea-god accordingly either Nereus, the husband of Doris, or Oceanus, the husband of Tethys. Though Catullus makes her grandparents give Thetis away, her parents are perhaps more likely here. That Nereus should be iconographically assimilated to Poseidon need cause no surprise, for the two were frequently confused. Of the remaining pair of onlookers the stately seated woman who watches Peleus across the whole width of the frieze has been generally accepted as Aphrodite; the sceptre would, it is true, suit Hera equally well, but the semi-nudity of the figure rules her out. Thus the queen of love herself presides over the meeting which she and her son have instigated: *coniugio quod fecit adest dea* (the goddess is present at the union which she has brought about).[18] As for the seated man at Thetis' feet, he is most probably Hermes, the god who brings fulfilment of lovers' desires and presides over the marriage bed. Hermes and Aphrodite were closely associated as match-makers in ancient cult and art.

It is unlikely that the subject of the frieze would have been

[15]Catullus, LXIV, 335-337.
[16]We catch a glimpse of another romantic version of the myth in Philostratus *Heroicus* XX, but it fits the frieze less well; for here the original roles are so far reversed that it is Thetis who makes the advances, and Peleus whose reluctance has to be overcome.
[17]Ovid *Metamorphoses* XI, 236 f. Ovid in his account of the wooing of Thetis by Peleus is of course committed to the wrestling-match by his general theme.
[18]Ovid *Metamorphoses* X.295.

arbitrarily chosen, without regard for the purpose or occasion for which the vase was made. The concept most obviously symbolized by the myth of Peleus and Thetis is, of course, that of happy marriage; and a writer of the third century A.D., Menander the Rhetorician, tells us that Peleus and Thetis shared with Dionysus and Ariadne the distinction of being the favourite themes for poems written to be recited at weddings.[19] The most probable inference from the subject of the frieze is, therefore, that the vase was designed to be a wedding-present; an auspicious and commemorative object rather than a functional one, though it may well have been filled with wine on occasion. The theory, first propagated by Teti (Appendix No. 2), that it was a cinerary urn, has less to commend it. Admittedly, Peleus and Thetis would not be out of place in a funerary context: in fact, their wedding-feast appears on a Roman sarcophagus[20], where it presumably symbolizes apotheosis in the after-life as a result of the soul's union with the divine. But there is no evidence at all to suggest that the Portland Vase was intended for funerary purposes. The story that it was found in a tomb is, as we have seen, pure invention; and the vase itself bears no significant resemblance to any known form of cinerary urn: glass cinerary urns were colourless, undecorated and lidded.[21]

TECHNIQUE, STYLE AND DATE

Both the blue glass of the body of the vase and the white glass of the frieze are alkali-lime-silica mixtures, the blue being due to the

[19]265, 8. Catullus's epyllion, which was doubtless composed for recitation at a wedding, combines both themes.
[20]in the Villa Albani, Rome. C. Robert. *Die antiken Sarkophag-Reliefs*, Vol. II, Berlin 1890, Pl. 1.
[21]Lest the Pompeian Blue Vase be cited as evidence to the contrary, it should perhaps be pointed out that the tomb in which it was 'discovered' was excavated in the presence of King Bomba, and the excavators had no doubt taken the normal precaution of furnishing it adequately before the royal visit. In all probability the vase had been found elsewhere (cf. Schulz *Annali dell'Instituto*, Rome, 1839, p. 87) and filled with ashes in imitation of the Portland Vase, then universally accepted as a cinerary urn.

addition of oxides of iron, manganese, copper and cobalt, the white to antimony calcium oxide.[22] The first step in the manufacture was to blow the blue glass body[23] and coat it with a layer of the white glass reaching up to a level just above the shoulder of the vase. To achieve this, the glass-blower may have dipped a partially inflated mass or paraison of the blue glass into a crucible containing a molten mixture of the white, thus 'gathering' the white layer; or he may have formed a 'cup' of white glass and then blown the blue glass into it.[24] Having 'cased' the blue glass in the white by one method or the other, he will then have brought the body to the required shape and size by further blowing and by rolling it on a marble slab or marver. The average thickness of the blue glass is about ⅛ inch (3 mm.). To blow a two-layered vessel as large as the Portland Vase must have called for considerable manipulative skill, but the ancient craftsman's chief difficulty was probably to prepare two differently coloured glasses with the same coefficient of contraction, an essential condition if they were not to crack or split apart on cooling.[25] After completing the body the glass-blower's last task was to fashion the handles from glass rods and attach them; their lower ends, which spring from the shoulder, were stuck to the white glass layer, their upper ends to the blue glass of the neck.

The vase was now handed over to a glass-engraver to carve the frieze, cut the ornament of the handles, and bring the whole to a finish. No doubt the frieze was copied from a model in wax or plaster, and the engraver will have begun by incising the outlines of the design on the white glass; then all the white glass will have been removed from the background so as to expose the blue; and lastly the figures and other features thereby left in

[22]W. E. S. Turner and H. P. Rooksby *Journal of the Society of Glass Technology*, Vol. XLIII, Sheffield, 1959, pp. 262-288.

[23]It has been suggested that the body might have been carved out of a solid block of glass, but elongated bubbles within the thickness of the wall prove that it was blown.

[24]On this method of 'casing' see Apsley Pellatt *Curiosities of Glass Making*, London, 1849, pp. 114-116.

[25]The best-known modern copy of the vase in glass, the Northwood-Pargeter copy now in the British Museum, split as a result of internal stresses, *Journal of the Society of Glass Technology*, Vol. VIII, 1924, pp. 85-92.

block relief will have been modelled in detail. The grooved treatment of the drapery and rocks reveals the use of the engraving wheel, which was probably also used for grinding away the background and other relatively coarse work; but for the more intricate and delicate passages more sensitive tools would have been needed, small chisels, files and gravers. The relief is uniformly low, the greatest thickness of the white layer not exceeding about one eighth of an inch; but by skilful modulation of the surface the engraver has succeeded in creating a convincing illusion of rounded volumes. In places, particularly in the foliage of the trees, the white glass has been cut so thin that the blue shows through, producing an atmospheric effect; while some details – the further side of the shrine, for example – are actually carved in the blue glass, the white having been removed altogether.

Both in the effects at which they aimed, and in the means by which they achieved them, the Portland Vase and other examples of the same technique were, of course, imitating cameos carved in layered stones such as agate or onyx: indeed in the seventeenth and eighteenth centuries the material of the Portland Vase was often mistaken for stone, an error finally refuted by Mariette who pointed out[26] that to find a natural stone with a white layer of the required size and regularity would be nothing short of a miracle. Cameo-carving in layered stones seems to have originated in Ptolemaic Alexandria; and since Alexandria was also one of the most important centres of ancient glass-making, it is a reasonable guess that 'cameo–glass', as it is usually called, was likewise an Alexandrian invention. The earliest known example of the technique points to the same conclusion: it is a fragment of a plaque in the Egyptian Department of the British Museum and shows a man's leg and part of a bull in a purely Egyptian style which cannot be later than the third century B.C. (Pl. IXb).[27] The white-on-blue blank for the plaque must have been moulded, since glass-blowing was not invented until about 50 B.C.; but the relief was unquestionably carved.

Cameo-glass which can be certainly ascribed to pre-Roman times is, however, rare and the bulk of what has survived probably dates from the early Roman imperial period. The two most

[26]P. J. Mariette *Traité des pierres gravées*, Paris, 1750.
[27]Egyptian Antiquities Reg. No. 16600.

notable specimens after the Portland Vase – the Blue Vase in Naples (Pl. XII), and the Auldjo Jug in the British Museum (Pl. XIII) – were found in Pompeii and must therefore be earlier than A.D. 79, the year of the eruption of Vesuvius which destroyed the city. The Blue Vase was probably made in the second quarter of the first century A.D.; the sparse, rather straggling garlands which hang above the vintaging and music-making putti are characteristic of this period, as are also the chiaroscuro effects caused by abrupt transitions between high and low relief. The sadly fragmentary Auldjo Jug must be contemporary: in fact its floral scrolls are so close in style to those of the vase that it may well be by the same hand. Though not so immediate, a relationship of some kind also clearly exists between the Blue Vase and the Portland Vase. We may note as a small but significant link connecting the two that the capital-like block of stone which lies askew on the ground at Thetis' feet on the Portland Vase (Pl. VII), reappears on the Blue Vase, where it is to be seen in front of the rocky couch on which the young banqueter reclines (Pl. XII). The same detail occurs on a true cameo in Naples[28] and it is tempting to speculate whether it might not be the mark of a particular workshop specializing in cameo-carving. However that may be, the Portland Vase must be rather earlier than the two Pompeian pieces. The cool elegance of its frieze, so different in mood from the crowded, 'busy' decoration of the Blue Vase, is characteristic of the reign of Augustus (27 B.C. – A.D. 14). Augustan, too, is the two-dimensionality of the composition. The figures are spaced out along a common ground-line with virtually no overlapping, so that each is sharply outlined against the background; and the whole scene appears to be taking place on a shallow stage in front of a curtain of darkness which veils every hint of distance, even the further side of the shrine and the further branches of the trees. Painting, from which cameo-carving evidently derived much of its inspiration, exhibits the same tendencies at the same time: that is to say, in the transitional period between the Second and Third Pompeian Styles. Here we find pictures in which the figures are confined to a narrow tract of foreground, each in isolation, while the background appears as if shrouded in mist, in which only the vaguely looming forms of the

[28]A. Furtwängler *Die antiken Gemmen*, Leipzig and Berlin, 1900, pl. LVIII, 9.

nearest trees and rocks are visible.[29] So far as we know, this style
of painting was confined to Italy, and it seems reasonable to infer
that the Portland Vase, which echoes it, was also made in that
country; but the craftsmen who blew and carved it may well have
been Alexandrians, for it is certain that Alexandrian glass-houses
were already established in Italy by the Augustan period.

THE DISC

The flat disc of cameo glass formerly fastened beneath the vase
(Pl. IXa) has a diameter of 4¾ inches (12·1 cm.) and shows the
upper part of a young man turned in profile to the right. He gazes
fixedly in front of him, inclining his head slightly forward, and
raises the forefinger of his right hand towards his chin in a
gesture which is used in classical art to express doubt or con-
sternation. His costume characterizes him as an Asiatic: a short-
sleeved tunic over a long-sleeved undergarment, a billowing
mantle fastened at the throat by a circular brooch, and a
'Phrygian' cap swathed in a diaphanous scarf, one end of which
hangs down the cheek. Above and behind him, the background
is filled with foliage; the leaves, which are partly carved in the
blue glass, appear to be those of a plane.

An Asiatic youth portrayed in a moment of perplexity can hardly
be other than Paris, the son of King Priam of Troy, called upon
to arbitrate between the rival charms of Hera, Athena and
Aphrodite. The myth of the Judgment of Paris told how at the
wedding-feast of Peleus and Thetis Eris (Strife) threw among the
guests a golden apple inscribed 'For the fairest'; whereupon
each of the three goddesses claimed it for herself. As none of the
other Olympians dared intervene in so invidious a dispute, Zeus
decided to refer it to Paris, the most handsome of mortal men, at
that time still a simple herdsman on Mount Ida. When Paris
saw the goddesses approach and learnt from Hermes, their
conductor, what was required of him, he was thrown into confusion, hardly daring to look on their dazzling beauty; still less,
by choosing one, to offend the other two. But Hermes pointed out

[29]A. Rumpf *Malerei und Zeichnung* (Handbuch der Archäologie, Sechste
Lieferung) Munich, 1953, p. 171 f.

that to disobey Zeus would be more dangerous still, so Paris took courage and agreed to judge the goddesses. Each of the three competitors tried to bribe their referee, Hera promising him royal power and Athena martial success. But Paris awarded the apple to Aphrodite, who offered him the most beautiful woman in the world for his wife; and with Aphrodite's help he seduced Helen, the wife of King Menelaos of Sparta, and so caused the Trojan War.

The fact that the subject of the disc is related to that of the vase must be a coincidence, for, as we have already mentioned, the disc cannot be the vase's original base. In the first place their colours do not match, the background of the disc being a much paler blue. Then, though the disc is probably also Augustan in date or not much later, it is evidently not by the same hand as the frieze: the face, for example, is quite differently modelled, especially the area of the lips and nostrils; and the pupil of the eye, blank on the vase, is here indicated. Lastly, the disc has plainly been cut down from a larger composition, for no ancient artist would have curtailed a figure or a tree in this arbitrary manner: no doubt the complete plaque included the three goddesses and Hermes.[30] In its present state the disc is pieced together from three fragments; since Doubleday's drawing (Pl. XVI) indicates the fractures, but does not show the fragments spaced out, the damage was presumably done before 1845. Perhaps the Duchess of Gordon was the culprit, but more probably the glass was already broken before the restorer decided to use it to patch the vase; the run of the fractures suggests that they originated in a larger surface. To attach the disc the restorer cut a shallow circular groove in its upper surface, into which the bottom of the vase was bedded; and he also incised a line round its vertical edge in a not very successful attempt to give the improvised base a moulded profile. Whether the disc was fitted in antiquity or at some time between the discovery of the vase and 1642, we have no means of telling.

[30]The composition perhaps resembled that of the stucco relief of the Judgment of Paris in the Tomb of the Pancratii at Rome, *Memoirs of the American Academy in Rome*, Vol. IV, Rome 1924, Pl. XXVII.

APPENDIX: OTHER INTERPRETATIONS

1. Bernardino Capitelli's engraving, of which the only known complete example is in the Topham collection at Eton College (Bn 15.89), has a caption in which the subject of the frieze is said to be 'the dream of Olympias while bearing Alexander the Great', presumably a confusion between the birth legends of Alexander the Great and Alexander Severus. Cf. Nos. 2 and 3 below.

2. Hieronymus Tetius (Girolamo Teti; the name is often wrongly given as Terzi) *Aedes Barberinae*, Rome, 1642, pp. 26–29. Teti interprets the first side of the vase (figures A–D) as referring to the birth of the emperor Alexander Severus, the second side (figures E–G) to his death: A = Alexander the Great, in whose temple Alexander Severus was born; B = Genius of connubial love; C = Mamaea, the mother of Alexander, with the purple dragon of which, according to Lampridius, she dreamt on the night of the emperor's birth; D = Aevum or Time; the young man E symbolizes the shortness of Alexander's reign; the woman F, expiring on a sarcophagus, his death; G, an elderly man (*sic*), his empire.

3. Michael Angelus Causeus (de la Chausse) *Romanum Museum sive Thesaurus Eruditae Antiquitatis*, Rome, 1690, p. 29 f. pll. 53–55. De la Chausse reports it as 'generally accepted' that the first side of the vase represents the congress of Zeus Ammon in the form of a snake with Olympias, the mother of Alexander the Great: A = a Genius; C = Olympias with the anguiform Zeus Ammon; D = Zeus Ammon in his proper shape. The legend that Olympias was visited by Ammon in snake-form arose from Alexander's visit to Siwa Oasis, where he was greeted as the son of Ammon; similar legends sprang up later about Alexander Severus (Appendix No. 2) and Augustus (Appendix No. 19). In the first and second (1707) editions of his work de la Chausse passes over the figures on the second side of the vase (E–G) in silence, but in the third (1746) they are tentatively identified as Muses.

4. Pietro Santi Bartoli *Gli antichi sepolchri*, Rome, 1697, p. XII, pll. 84–86. Underworld scenes: C = Proserpina; E = Pluto; G = Proserpine. Bartoli is the first to assert that the vase was found, enclosed in the so called 'sarcophagus of Alexander Severus', in the tomb under the Monte del Grano on the outskirts of Rome.

5. B. de Montfaucon *L'antiquité expliquée*, Paris, 1722, Vol. V, p. 56, pl. 19. Mistaking the creature associated with C for a swan, Montfaucon identifies her as Leda (Zeus assumed the form of a swan in order to ravish Leda). D = Zeus in his proper form.

6. Ridolfino Venuti *Spiegazione de' bassirilievi dell' urna sepolcrale detta d'Alessandro Severo*, Rome, 1756, pp. 41–47, pl. IV. The Judgment of

Paris: A = Paris; B = Cupid; C = Discordia with snake; D = Jupiter (Zeus); E = Venus (Aphrodite); F = Minerva (Athena); G = Juno (Hera). Despite the absurdity of this interpretation, which involves changing the sex of E from male to female, it must be said in Venuti's defence that he is the first, and until L. Polacco (Appendix No. 20) the only, person to see that the two sides of the vase constitute a single scene; and he also correctly identifies the figure on the disc as Paris.

7. J. J. Winckelmann *Geschichte der Kunst des Altertums*, Vienna, 1776, Part II, p. 861 f. In a brief reference to the vase Winckelmann identifies A and C as Peleus and Thetis, the creature associated with C being a snake and symbolizing the transformations Thetis underwent while wrestling with Peleus. By making C the object of A's advances Winckelmann originated an error which was to vitiate most subsequent interpretations of the frieze.

8. P. d'Hancarville *Recherches sur l'origine, l'esprit et les progrès des arts de la Grèce*, London, 1785, Vol. II, pp. 142–160 (note), pll. 9–11. D'Hancarville is scornful of previous attempts at interpretation: 'cependant il s'est trouvé des gens capables de digérer ces extravagances, & de les prendre pour des raisons, comme Saturne digéroit les pierres qu'on lui faisoit prendre pour ses enfants. J'aimeroit autant dire de ce vase, qu'ayant servi a des *morts*, son bas-relief represente la mère du genre humain, dont le péché introduisit la *mort* dans le monde. Elle a près d'elle le *Serpent* qui la séduisit; elle entraine dans sa *chute* le premier homme qu'elle *tire par le bras:* Dieu, dans sa colère, *juge & punit* leur désobeissance. On le voit au pied du *figuier* dont la feuille servit a couvrir la nudité des premiers pécheurs. Les *arbres* sont ici ceux du jardin d'Eden, dont la *porte*, qui surement étoit d'ordre *Dorique* puisque c'est le plus ancien de tous les ordres, se voit à l'entrée du paradis terrestre. Enfin l'Ange préposé à sa garde, plane dans les airs: on y reconnoit celui que dépeint Milton, mais il porte un *flambeau* au lieu d'*epée flamboyante* que ce poète lui met a la main. Ainsi ce vase fut fait vers le temps d'Adam ou d'Olivier Cromwel'.

But d'Hancarville's own interpretation of the frieze as showing underworld scenes hardly deserves to be taken more seriously: A = Orpheus; C = Eurydice with the snake that killed her; D = Pluto; E = Pollux with Castor in the form of a pillar; F = Alcestis; G = Tyro. The *Göttingische Anzeigen* of 1786 not unfairly calls this interpretation 'the most forced and improbable in the world'.

9. J. G. King *Archaeologia*, Vol. VIII, London, 1787, pp. 307–315. The first side of the vase, according to King, is 'an allusion to the birth of Alexander the Great under which is typified the birth of Alexander Severus': A = Alexander the Great/Alexander Severus; C = Olympias/Mamaea; D = Jupiter. On the second side E = Alexander Severus sitting on a bath, which symbolizes the *thermae* built by the emperor; F = Mamaea; G = Constancy.

10. C. Marsh *Archaeologia*, Vol. VIII, London, 1787, pp. 316–320. Marsh sees the frieze as presenting, somewhat in the manner of Hogarth, 'scattered features of well-known history, satyrically sketched out . . . to lash a luxurious emperor, addicted to the most shameful vices, and to praise a virtuous one.' The luxurious emperor, Heliogabalus (E), 'sits with his garment loose, in attitude slothful, obscene and libidinous. At his feet female or connubial love (F) lies sorrowful . . . We read of Augusta Paula, a most beautiful woman, rejected and repudiated by that monster of impurity; and we know the causes of that repudiation . . . On the right of the woman is a female monitor (G), divination, revolving many things in her mind, fixed in purpose, leaning firmly, perhaps, on an augural lituus, just going to give a response to the tyrant, or, like another Syrian priestess, ready to denounce his death'. Virtue being less interesting than vice, Marsh has less to say about the other side of the vase, on which he follows Teti: A = Alexander Severus, 'the distributor of oil, an enemy to effeminacy and smoke-selling, attached to dreams and divination'; C = Mamaea; D = Jupiter.

11. Josiah Wedgwood, 1790, quoted in *The Portland Vase* published by Josiah Wedgwood and Sons Ltd., Etruria, Stoke-on-Trent, 1907, pp. 6–10. Wedgwood thought that the frieze represented death and the entrance of the soul into Elysium: the reclining woman (F) with an inverted torch is an emblem of death; 'the column behind . . .(E) . . . with its capital thrown down at the feet of this emblem of death may denote that the person deceased was the head of a great family, as so costly an urn would only be purchased by persons of the first rank. The sceptre in the left hand of . . . (G) . . . may be an emblem of the authority of the deceased . . . The other side of the vase appears to be a separate picture in continuation of the same subject, and flattering to the memory of the deceased, representing his entrance under the figure of a young man (A) into Elysium. A gate or portico it is well known signifies the passage from the present state of our existence to the future. The timidity with which the new guest takes his first steps out of this portal, his holding fast to his garment, beautifully denotes the reluctance with which he puts off his corporeal existence. As on the first side the central and principal figure was typical of death, so on the obverse side the chief figure (C) holds the serpent, the symbol of immortal life. She takes the shade tenderly by the hand, and by her look and action encourages him to come forward; while Cupid (B), a lighted torch in his hand, directs his path towards Pluto (D), who awaits him, with thoughtful mien'.

12. Erasmus Darwin *The Botanic Garden*, London, 1791, Part I (The Economy of Vegetation), Canto II, 321–340.

> *Here* by fall'n columns and disjoin'd arcades,
> On mouldering stones, beneath deciduous shades,
> Sits HUMANKIND (E and G) in hieroglyphic state,
> Serious and pondering on their changeful state;
> While with inverted torch, and swimming eyes,

Sinks the fair shade of MORTAL LIFE (F), and dies.
There the pale GHOST (A) through Death's wide portal bends
His timid feet, the dusky steep descends;
With smiles assuasive LOVE DIVINE (B) invites,
Guides on broad wing, with torch uplifted lights;
IMMORTAL LIFE (C), her hand extending, courts
The lingering form, his tottering steps supports;
Leads on to Pluto's (D?) realms the dreary way,
And gives him trembling to Elysian day.
Beneath, in sacred robes the Priestess dress'd,
The coif close-hooded, and the fluttering vest,
With pointing finger guides the initiate youth,
Unweaves the many-coloured veil of Truth,
Drives the profane from Mystery's bolted door,
And Silence guards the Eleusinian lore.

The identification of IMMORTAL LIFE, the author says (Additional note XXII, p. 55), 'is evinced by her fondling between her knees a large and playful serpent, which from its annually renewing its external skin has from great antiquity, even as early as the fable of Prometheus, been esteemed an emblem of renovated youth'.

13. J. Millingen *Transactions of the Royal Society of Literature*, Vol. I, 2, London, 1829, pp. 99–105. An elaboration of Winckelmann's interpretation (Appendix No. 7): A = Peleus; C = Thetis with a marine serpent; D = Neptune (Poesidon); E = Peleus; F = Thetis; G = a personification of Mount Pelion.

14. T. Windus *A new elucidation of the subjects on the celebrated Portland Vase*, London, 1845. 'Conceiving that the character of one of the male figures (called by some Pluto, by others Neptune) (D) had a medical appearance similar to that of Esculapius or Hippocrates, on the coins of Cos, I resorted to the biographies of the ancient Greek and Roman physicians. When I came to that of Galen, the whole allegory blazed on me at once in union with my favourite hypothesis – the sexes correct – and all the attributes, recording an event which occurred in the second century; from the excitement I exclaimed with all the ardour of Archimedes, EUREKA! EUREKA!!'. The event referred to by Windus was a famous cure which Galen achieved in the case of one of the daughters of the emperor Marcus Aurelius, either Lucilla or Fadilla. The girl had fallen ill of a mysterious disease which seemed incurable until at length Galen was called in. Diagnosing that she was suffering from a secret passion for a rope-dancer named Pylades, the learned physician prescribed a visit from the cause of her malady, which at once restored the patient. On one side of the vase Lucilla or Fadilla (F) pines away between Marcus Aurelius (E) and Faustina, her mother (G); on the other, the restored Lucilla or Fadilla (C), 'with the gyrating Hygeian Serpent, emblem of healing', welcomes the advancing rope-dancer (A), while Galen (D) looks on. Galen's features are also to be recognized in the Pan's masks of the handles, which are 'face-skins' composed of leeches.

15. W. Watkiss Lloyd *Classical Museum* Vol. VI, London, 1849, pp. 253–278. Lloyd follows Millingen (Appendix No. 13) in maintaining that Peleus and Thetis are repeated on each side of the vase; but he is the first to draw attention to Catullus *Carmen* LXIV and Philostratus *Heroicus* XX as evidence of the existence of romantic versions of their myth in which the wrestling match played no part.

16. C. T. Pyl *De Medeae Fabula*, Berlin, 1850, p. 20. E = Jason; F = Medea; G = Aphrodite.

17. W. Klein *Euphronios*, Vienna, 1879, p. 68, note 2. A = Theseus approaching the palace of Poseidon under the sea to retrieve the ring of King Minos; C = Amphitrite; D = Poseidon.

18. F. Granger, in a letter to Messrs Christie, Manson and Woods (quoted in *The Times* and *The Morning Post* of 30th March, 1929) 'The figures may even have a Christian significance and be symbolical of Birth, Death and Immortality. Alexander Severus in the spirit of Neo-Platonism combined many worships . . . On one side Mammaea (C) is greeted by Alexander the Great (A) on the steps of his temple and the scene indicates the mysterious birth of Alexander Severus . . . On the other side Mammaea (F) in the attitude of the sleeping Ariadne of the Vatican . . . holds an inverted torch which might indicate sleep. But the Fate, Clotho (G), with her spindle, seated behind Mammaea, gives a funeral meaning to the torch. The base of the vase represents a youth in a Phrygian cap with his fingers to his lips, probably Orpheus on his mysterious errand, the descent into Hell. Him an imaginative reader might well identify with Christ . . .'

19. Erika Simon *Die Portlandvase*, Mainz, 1953. The writer argues that the frieze represents a legend that the emperor Augustus was the son of Apollo, who had visited his mother, Atia, in the form of a snake (cf. Appendix No. 3). The myth is recorded by Suetonius (*De Vita Caesarum* II, 94) from the *Theologoumena* of Asklepiades of Mendes. Figures E–G represent the first meeting between Apollo and Atia: E = Apollo, who also incorporates the Roman deities Veiovis and Terminus; F = Atia; G = Venus Genetrix. Figures A–D represent the subsequent union of Apollo and Atia: A = Apollo-Veiovis, whose features resemble those of Augustus; C = Atia with Apollo in the form of a snake; D = Romulus-Quirinus. The Pan's masks beneath the handles represent Capricorn, the constellation under which Augustus was born.

20. L. Polacco *Athenaeum* New Series, Vol. XXXVI, Pavia, 1958, pp. 123–141. The first correct interpretation of the *action* of the frieze. Polacco points out that the two sides of the vase constitute a single scene, F, not C, being the object of A's advances. But he accepts the identifications proposed by Simon (Appendix No. 19) for the attendant figures, and suggests that the whole probably celebrates the marriage of Julia, the daughter of Augustus, to his nephew, C. Claudius Marcellus

(23 B.C.): A = Marcellus; C = Atia; D = Romulus-Quirinus; E = Apollo-Veiovis-Terminus; F = Julia; G = Venus Genetrix.

21. H. Möbius *Die Reliefs der Portlandvase und das antike Dreifigurenbild* (Bayerische Akademie der Wissenschaften, Philosophisch-historische Klasse, Abhandlungen, Neue Folge, Heft 61), Munich, 1965. A–D as Klein (Appendix No. 17); E = Theseus, F = Ariadne, G = Aphrodite.

22. F. Bastet *Bulletin Antieke Beschaving*, Vol. XLI, 1966, takes the two sides together as representing Ariadne (F) and Dionysus (A) on Naxos. C = Naxos (?), D = Poseidon, E = Apollo (?), G = Aphrodite.

23. B. Ashmole *Journal of Hellenic Studies*, Vol. LXXXVII, 1967, pp. 1–17. A = Peleus, C = Thetis, D = Poseidon. E and F are Achilles and Helen on the White Isle, with Aphrodite, G.

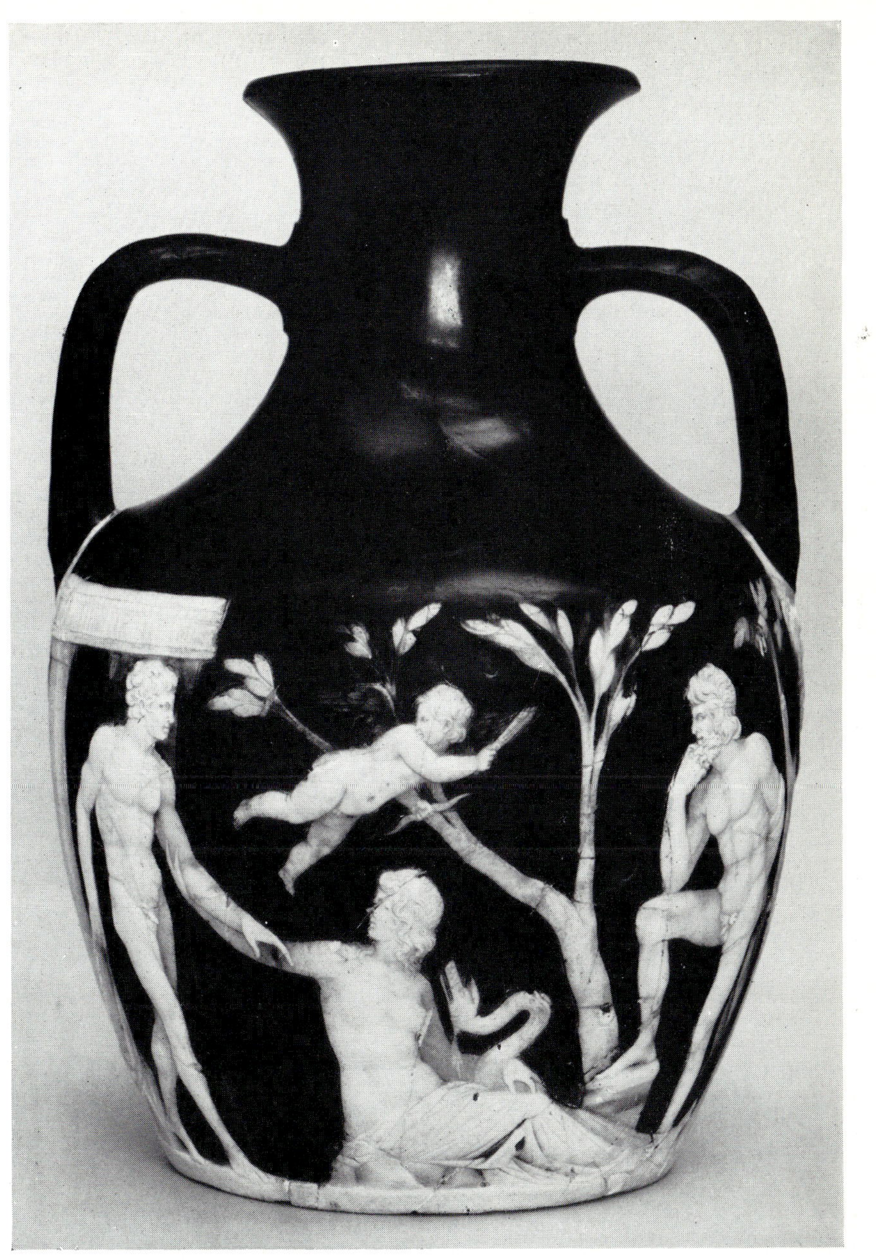

PLATE I   Whole Vase, figures A—D

33

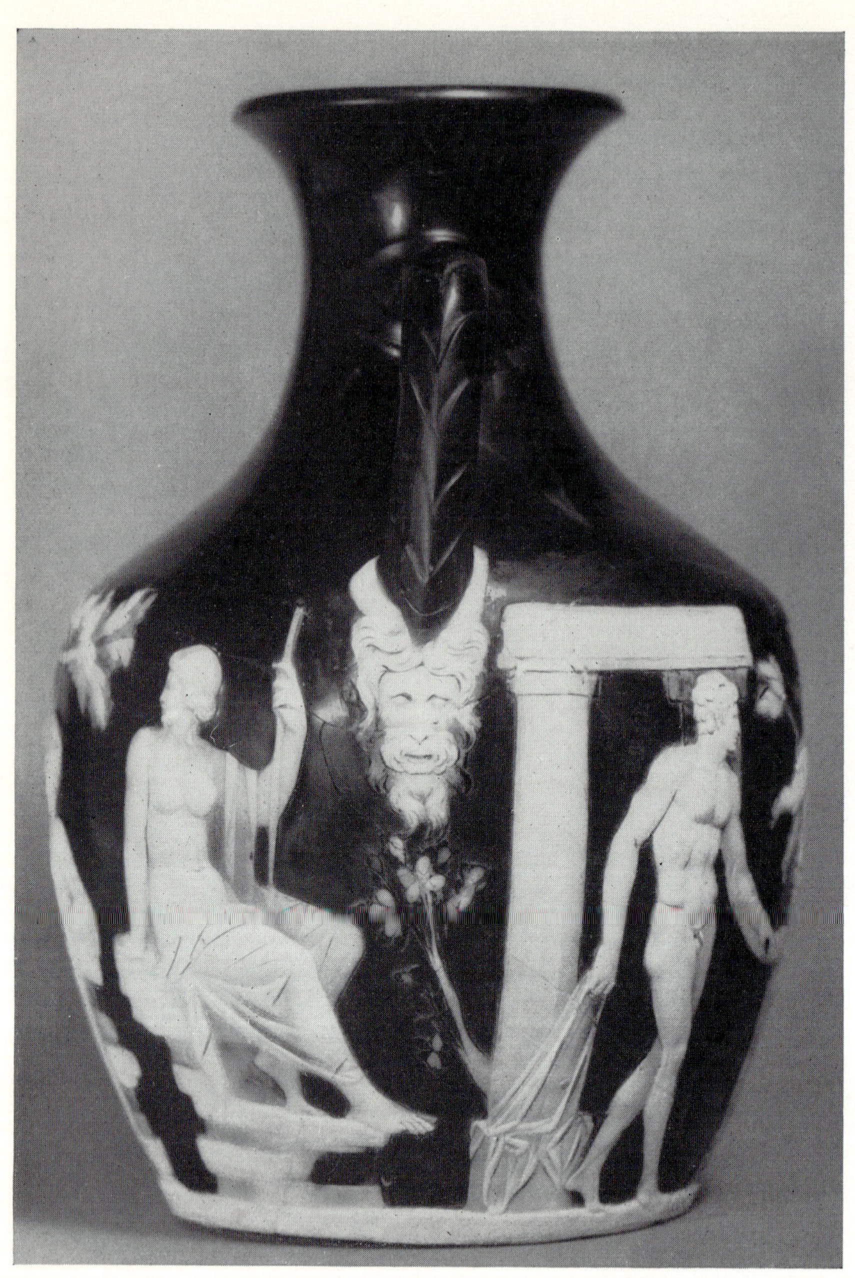

PLATE II Whole Vase, figures G and A

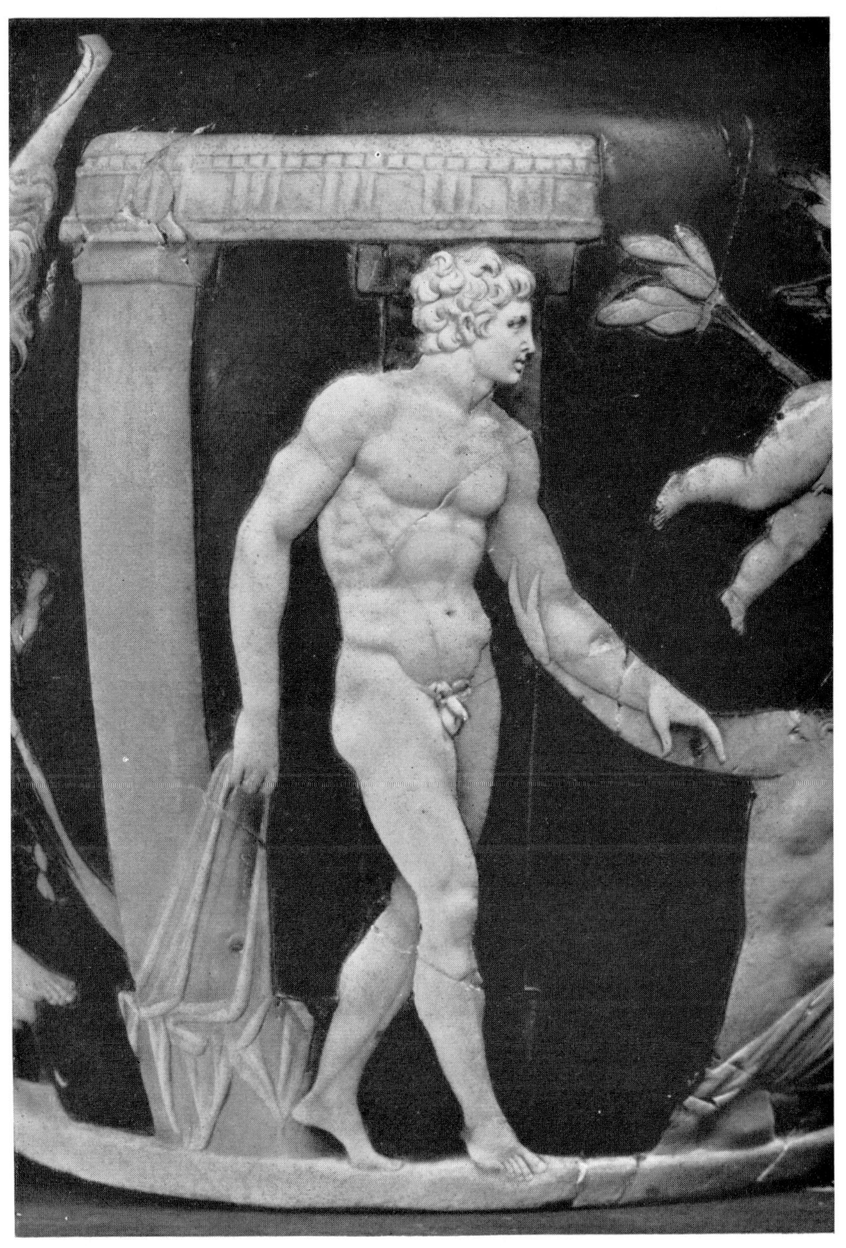

PLATE III   Detail, figure A

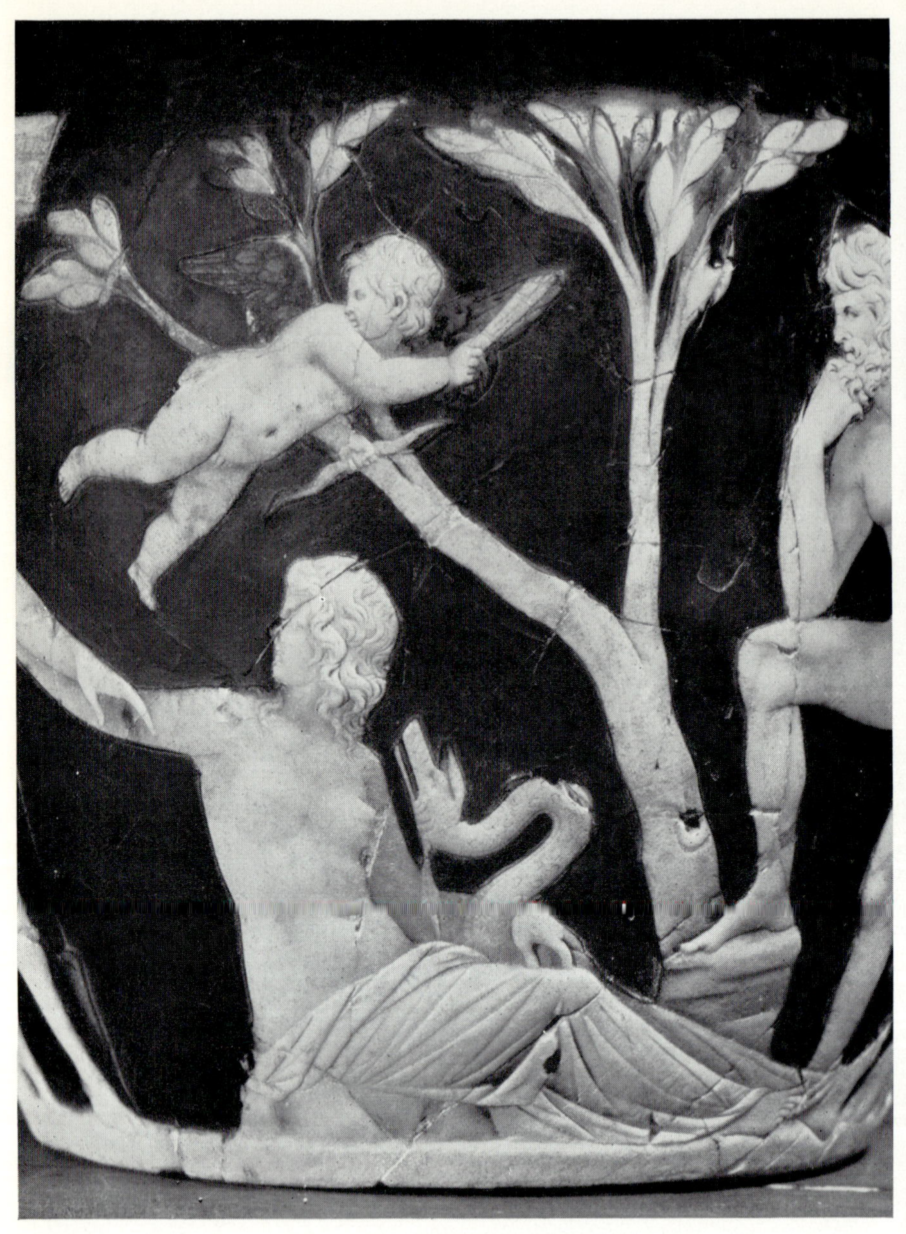

PLATE IV   Detail, figures B and C

36

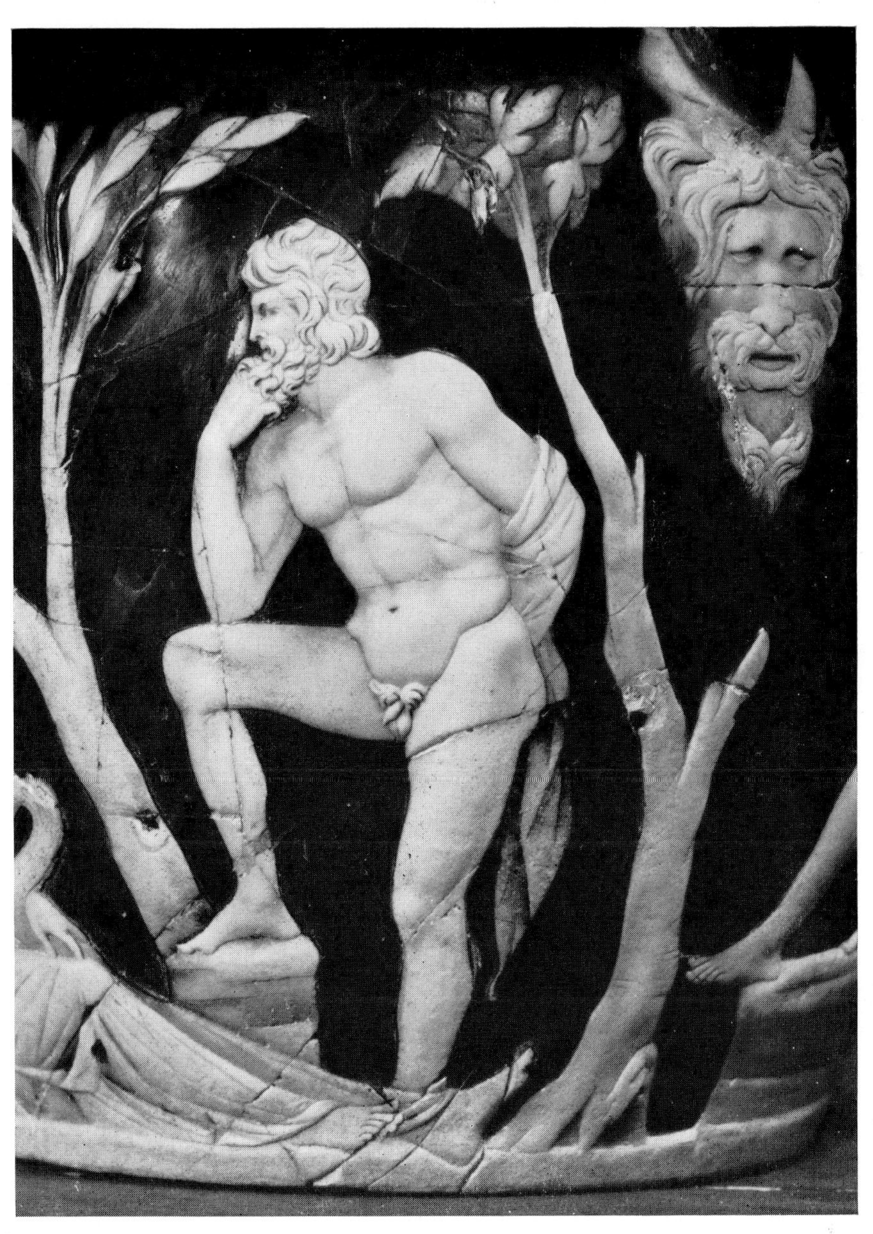

PLATE V   Detail, figure D

37

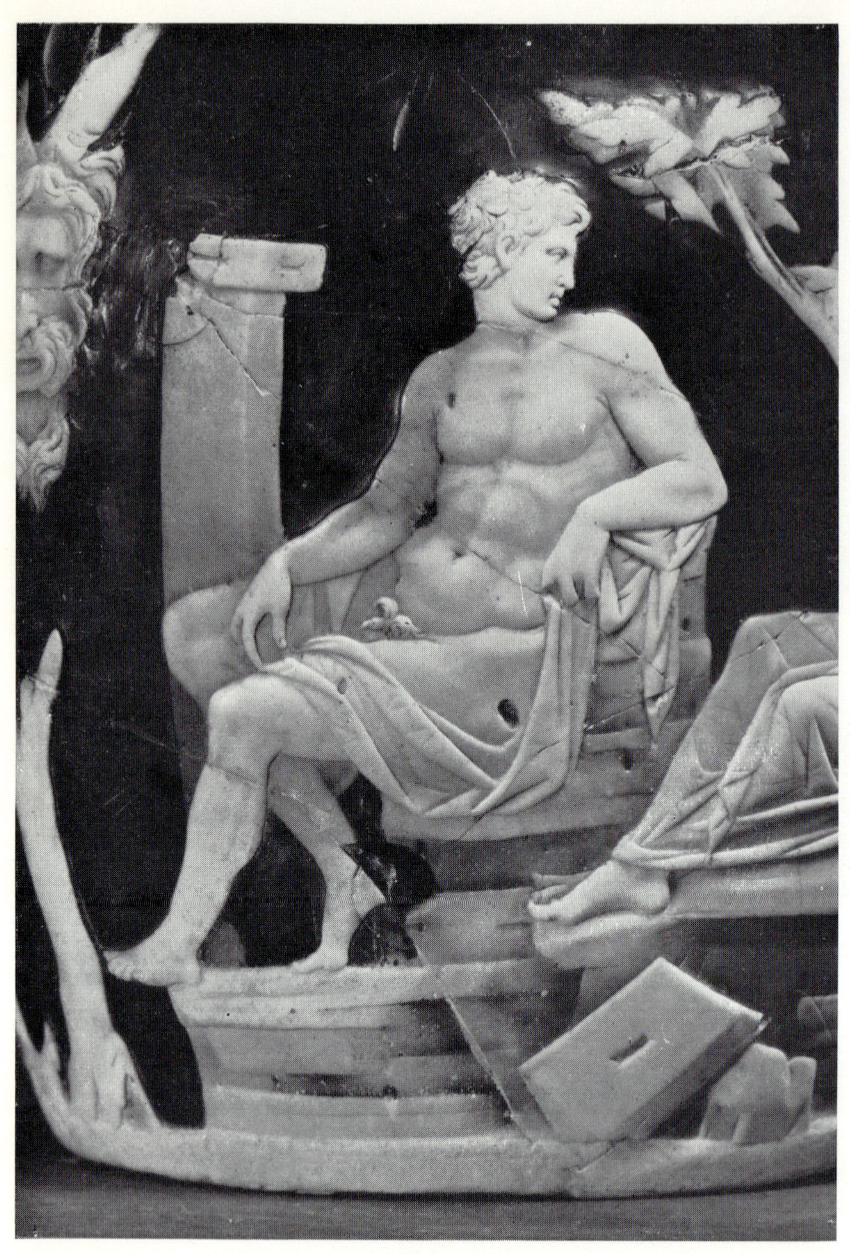

PLATE VI   Detail, figure E

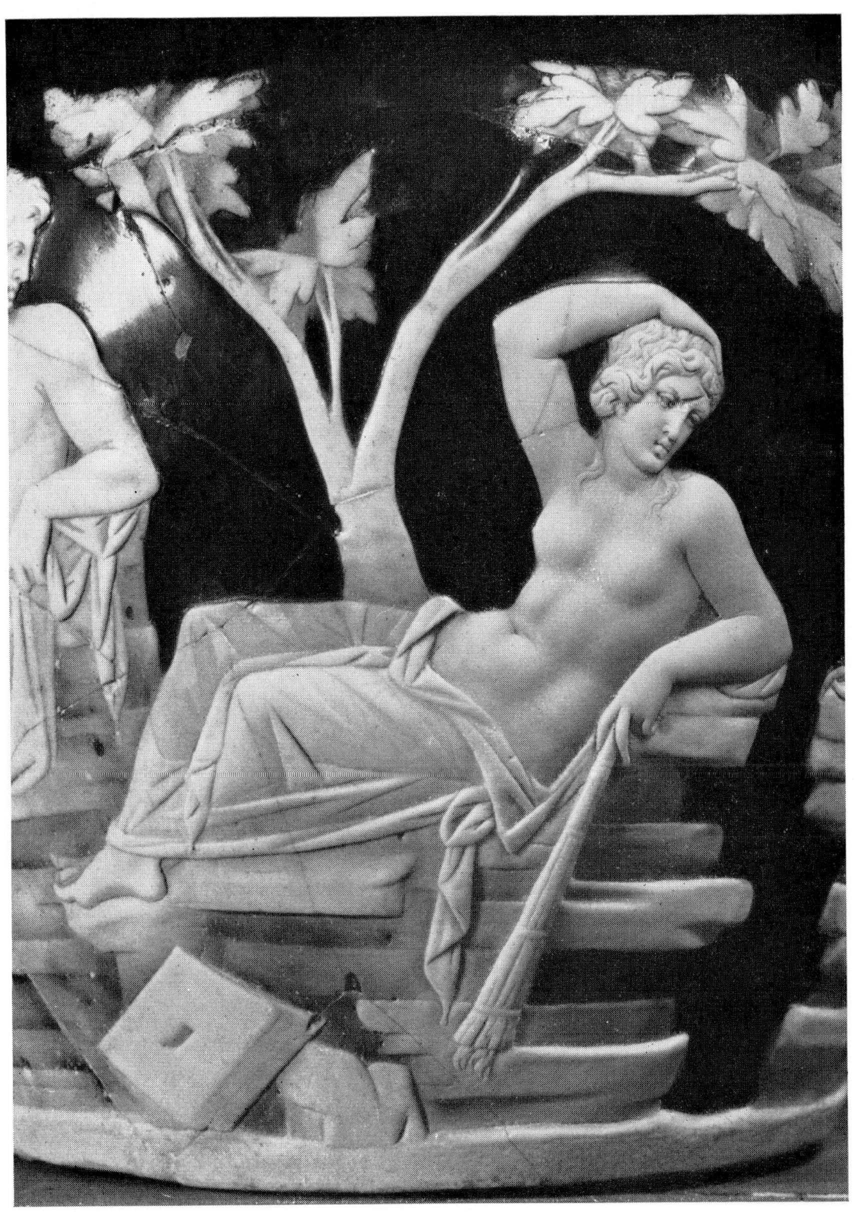

PLATE VII   Detail, figure F

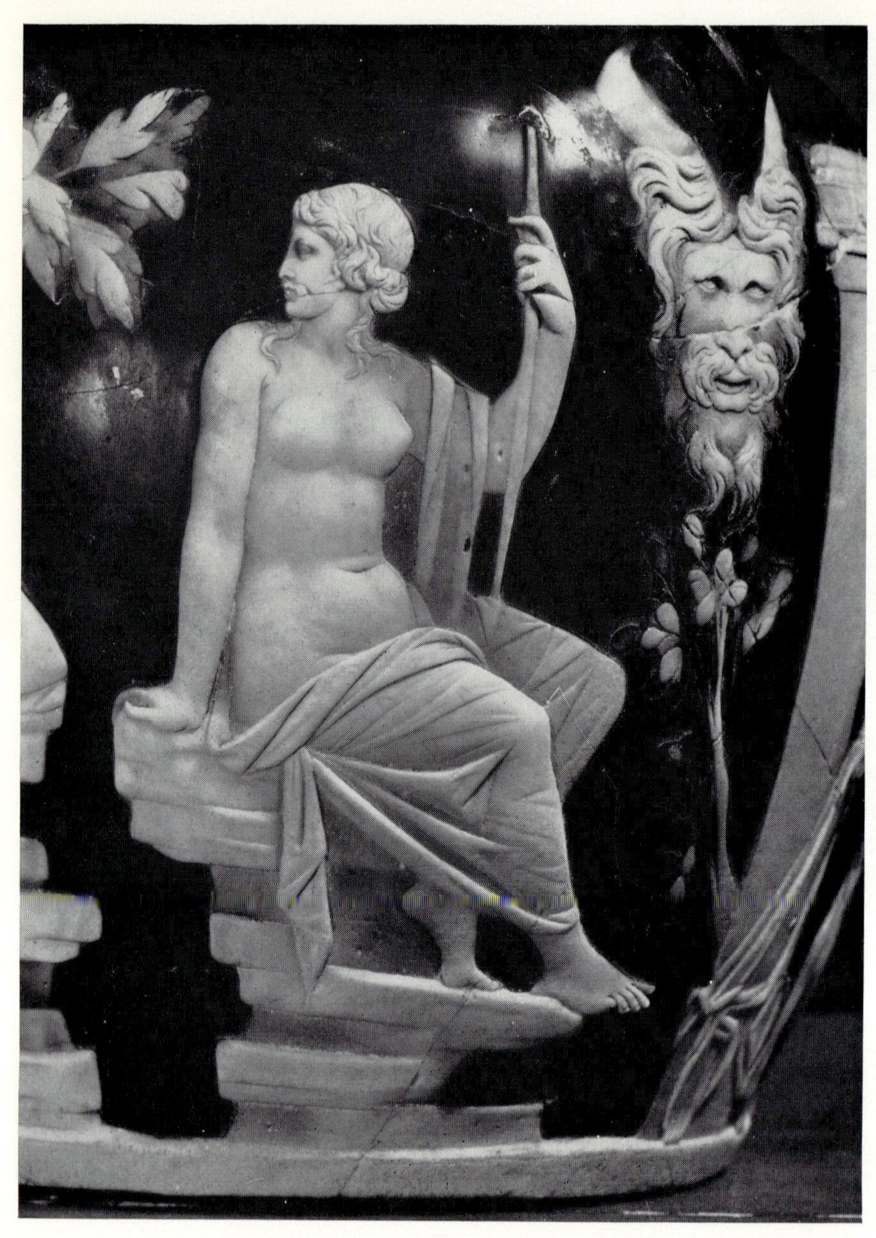

PLATE VIII   Detail, figure G

40

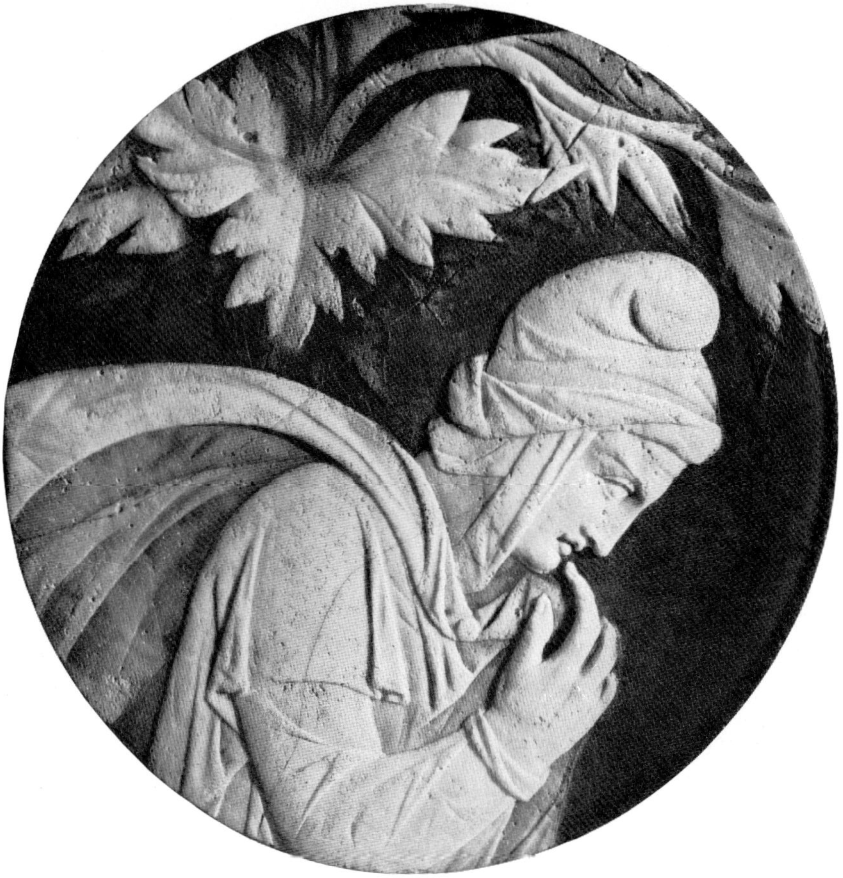

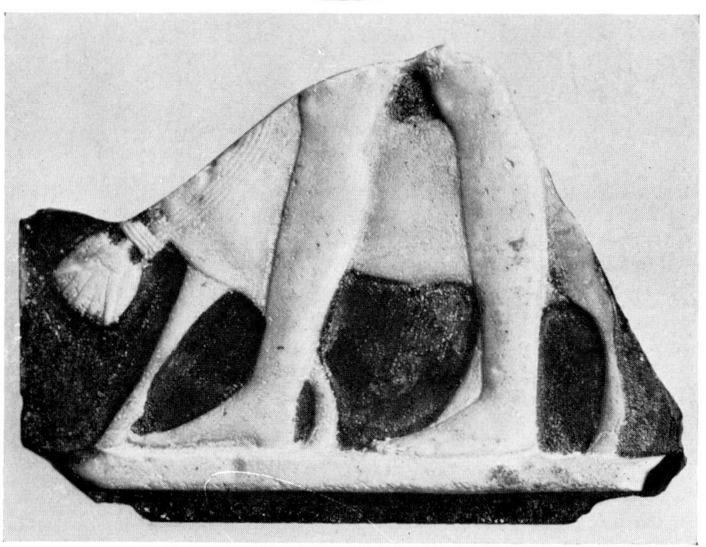

PLATE IX   (a) Disc formerly fastened beneath the Portland Vase
(b) Fragment of cameo glass plaque (British Museum)

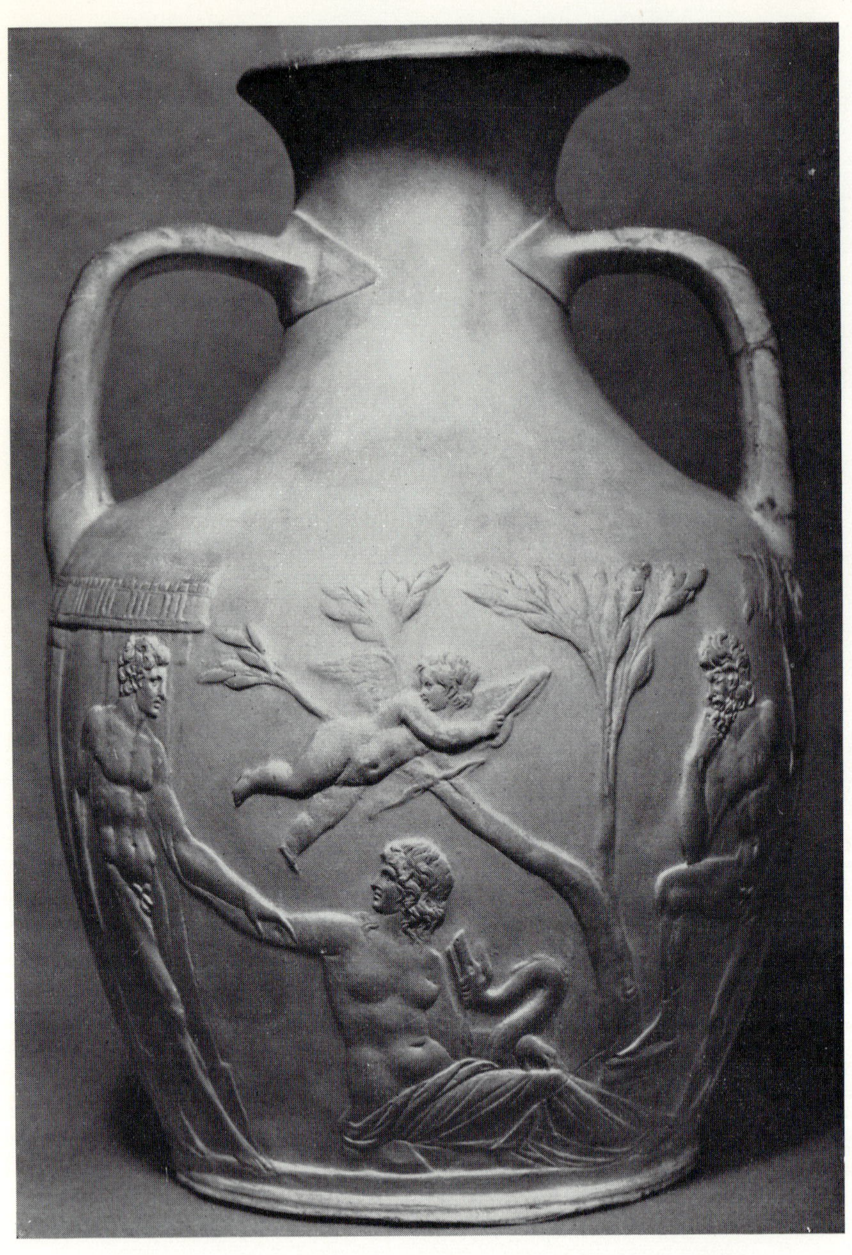

PLATE X   Plaster cast of the Portland Vase by Pichler and
Tassie, ca 1780 (British Museum), figures A—D

42

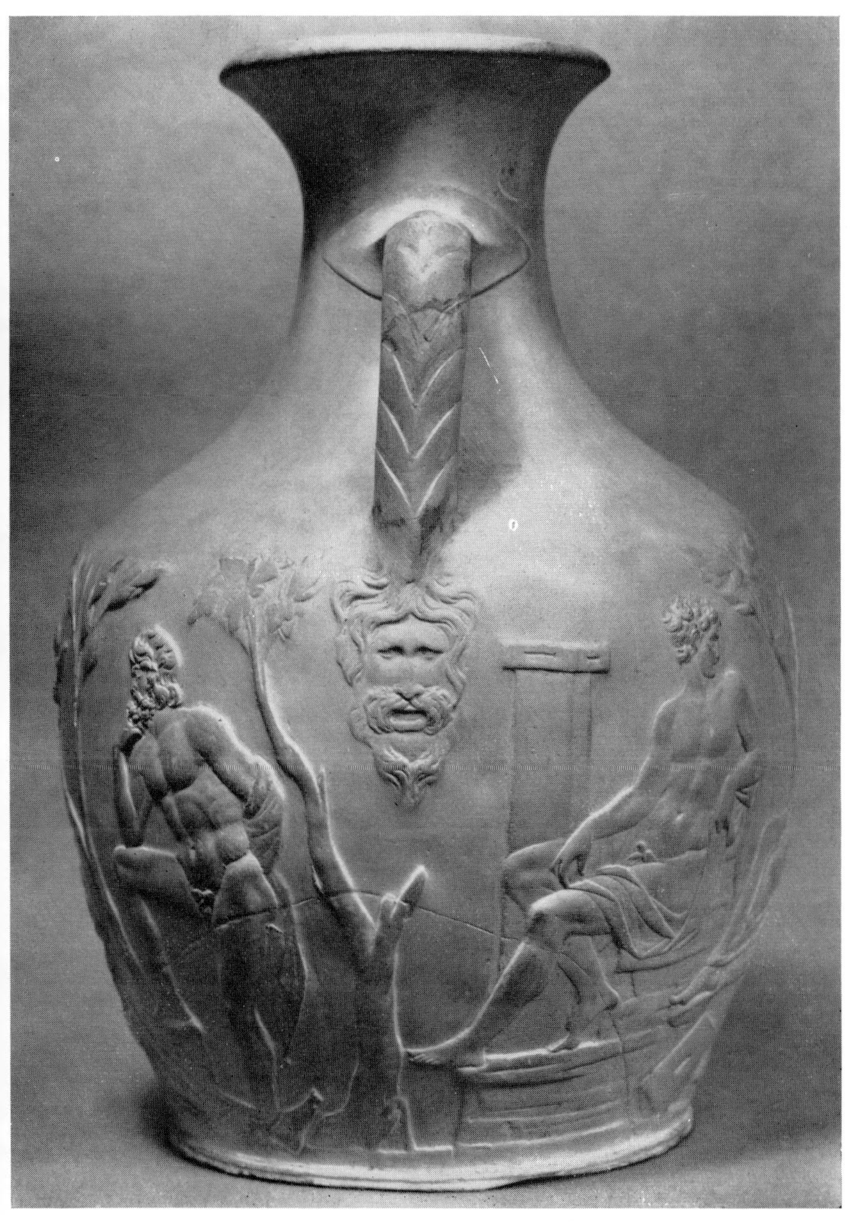

PLATE XI   Plaster cast of the Portland Vase, figures D and E

43

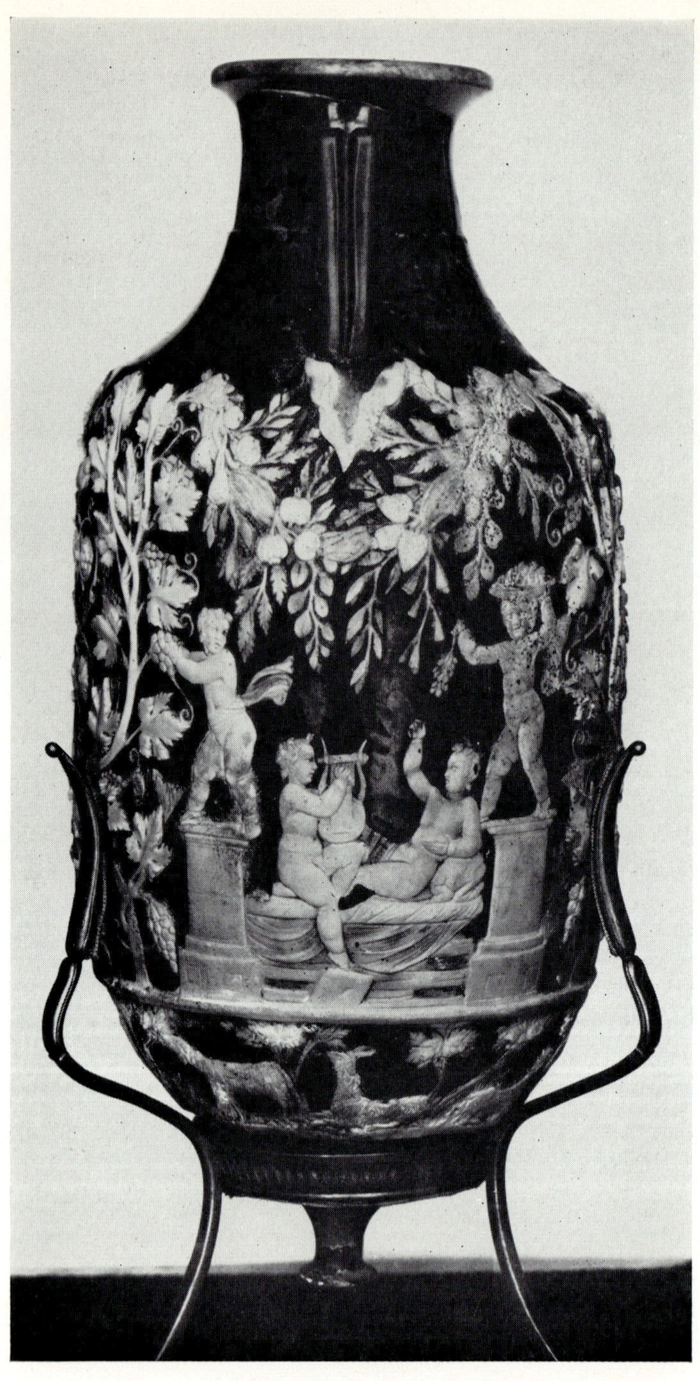

PLATE XII   The Blue Vase (National Museum, Naples)

44

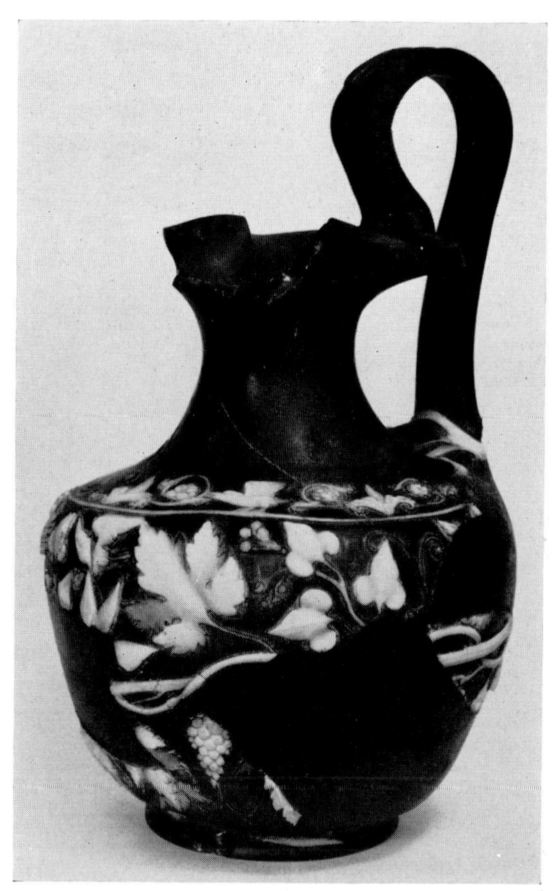

PLATE XIII   The Auldjo Jug (British Museum)

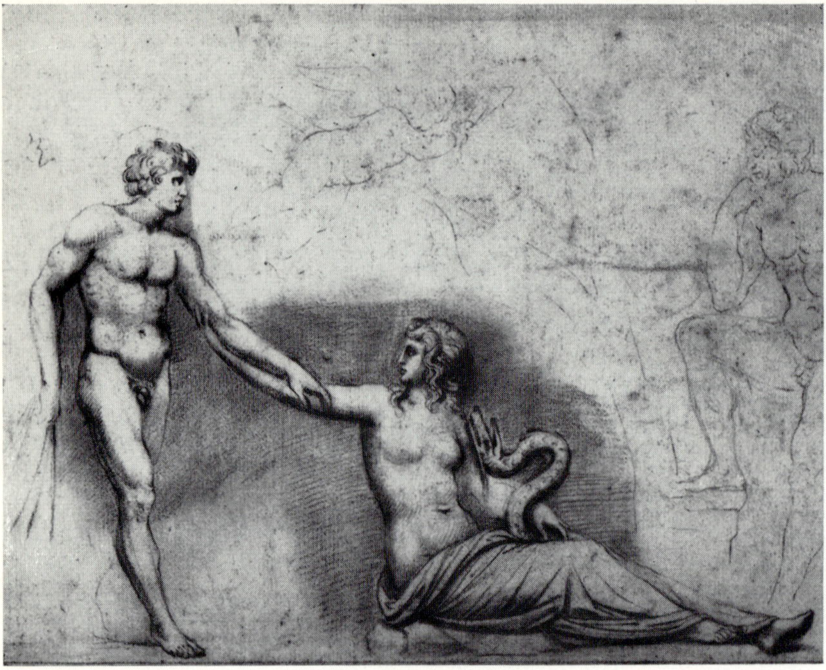

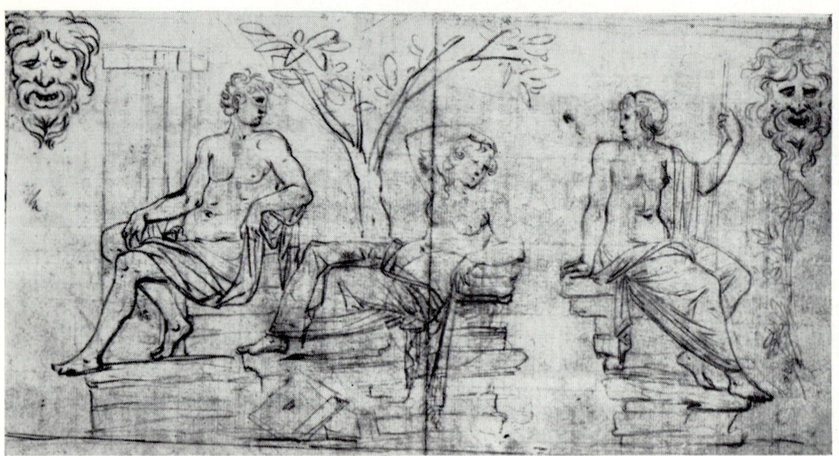

PLATE XIV Two drawings of the Portland Vase from Cassiano dal Pozzo's *Museum Chartaceum* (British Museum)

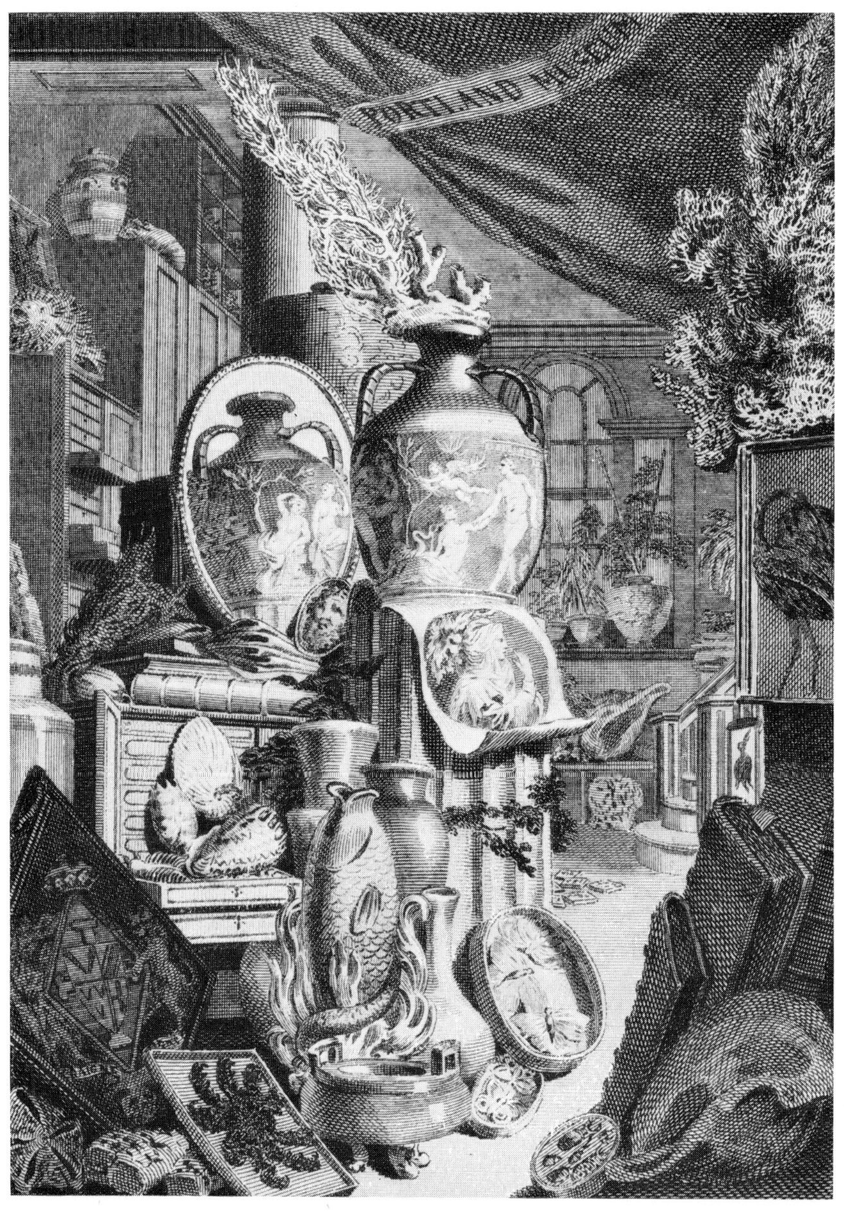

PLATE XV 'The Portland Museum', frontispiece to Mr Skinner
and Co.'s sale catalogue, 24 April – 7th June 1786

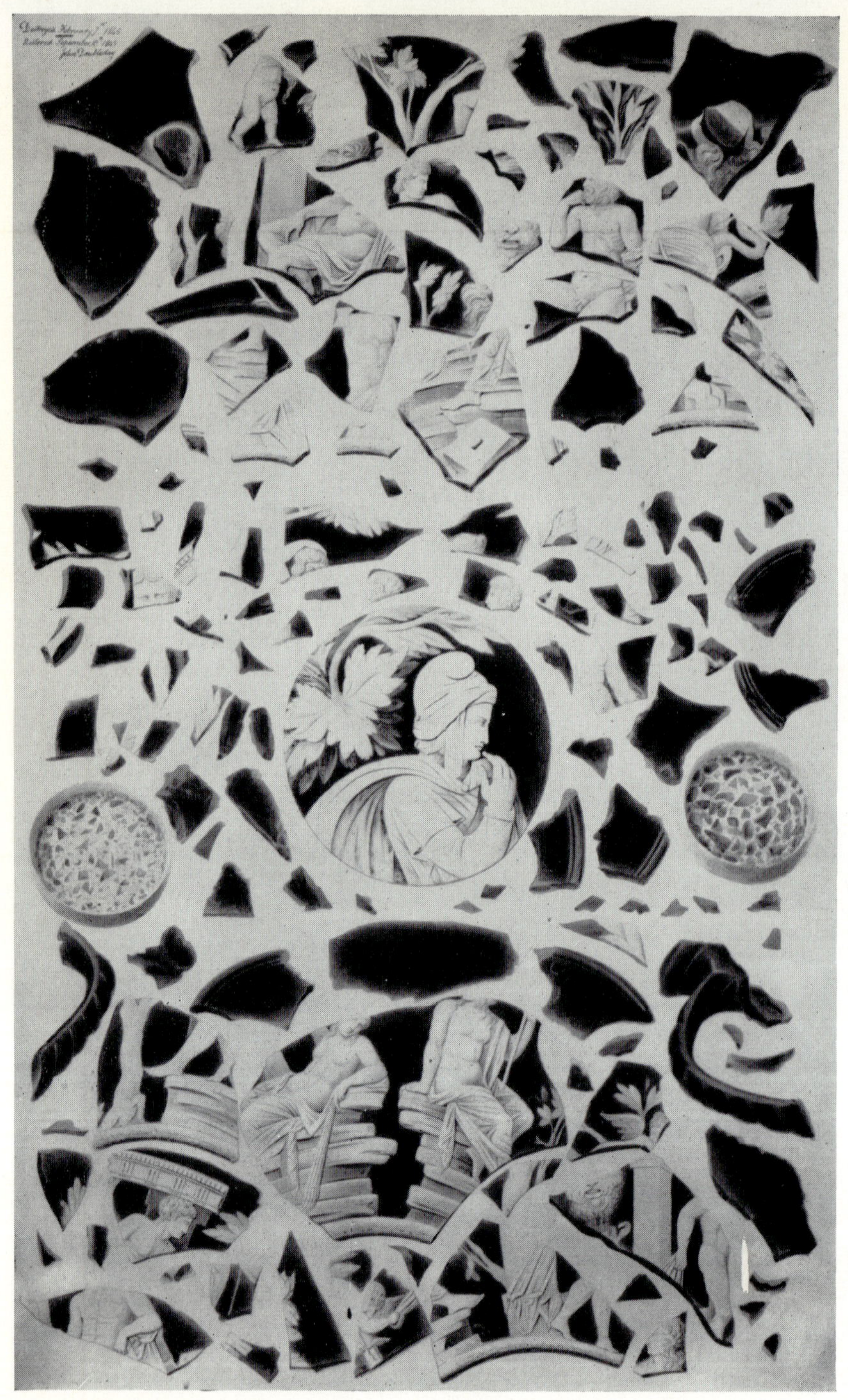

PLATE XVI   Drawing by John Doubleday of the fragments of the
Portland Vase after its destruction on 7th February 1845

48